The $163 Lightbulb

How Albany's Mandates Drive Up Your Local Taxes

By Robert B. Ward

The Public Policy Institute of New York State, Inc.

November 1999

Published by The Public Policy Institute, Albany, New York
November 1999

The Public Policy Institute is a research and educational organization affili-
ated with The Business Council of New York State, Inc., the state's largest
broad-based business group. The Institute's mission is to analyze the public-
policy choices facing New York State from a private-sector perspective, and to
make a constructive contribution to the public dialogue in the state. The Institute is supported by contributions from employers and individuals across
New York. It is classified as a Section 501(c)(3) organization under the Internal Revenue Code of 1954.

*Note: Nothing written herein is to be construed as an attempt to aid, or hinder,
the passage of any specific bill before Congress or the New York State Legislature.*

Additional copies of this book are available for $10 each,
directly from the Institute:

**The Public Policy Institute
of New York State, Inc.**
152 Washington Avenue
Albany, New York 12210-2289
518/465-7511
http://www.ppinys.org

The Public Policy Institute

Cover design and book composition
  by Associated Creative Services, Inc., Albany, New York.

Cover photograph of the Empire State Plaza
  by William DeMichele

Table of Contents

Medicaid and other social-service costs in New York are out of control. With real reform of social services administration, long-term care and other costs, county property taxes could be cut by two-thirds or more.

Too much interference from Albany means that the people running public schools in New York have too little authority to allocate essential resources, and to insist on well-qualified teachers and administrators.

The notorious Wicks Law, and prevailing-wage mandates that are not as well known, drive taxpayers' costs for construction needlessly high—at the same time they create harmful delays in building new schools and other projects.

The civil service system was created to make government better—but now it often stands in the way of quality public services. In addition, binding arbitration and other aspects of the state's Taylor Law are badly in need of reform.

Lawsuits, often frivolous, drain hundreds of millions of local tax dollars every year in New York because of unfair state laws. And volunteer services are endangered, in part by heavy-handed state mandates.

Strong action by Governor Pataki and the Legislature to eliminate harmful mandates on local governments and school districts could save taxpayers $5 billion or more each year—while improving education and other vital services.

Introduction

How Albany's Mandates Drive Up Your Local Taxes

Imagine if the Governor and the Legislature enacted laws that required your county, city and school district to add 25 percent or more to the cost of constructing a new building, for no improvement in quality.

Taxpayers would be furious—and rightfully so.

Repealing mandates will improve vital public services—and save taxpayers millions of dollars.

How about if Albany announced it would force City Hall to spend $163 of taxpayers' money on changing a traffic light bulb?

Or, imagine a law that makes public schools keep incompetent or even criminal teachers and principals on the job, and on the payroll, while dismissal proceedings drag on literally for years.

You'll hear no announcements bragging about these laws—but, the fact is, they're all on the books in New York State, and have been for years.

New York State has revolutionized its business climate in recent years, cutting taxes and rolling back regulatory red tape to allow the private sector to thrive. These hard-won changes reflected a recognition that hurdles set up by Albany were making it impossible for businesses in the Empire State to produce economic growth and new jobs at the pace of those in other states. And the changes are paying off: Statewide, New York has added more than half a million jobs in the second half of the 1990s.

But in many ways, state government's approach to municipalities and school districts has remained the same as its traditional approach to businesses: Impose heavy costs, stifle innovation with bureaucratic red tape, and ignore the damage that well-intended policies from Albany create out in the real world. In fact, many of those mandates were enacted from the 1960s to the early 1990s; during much of that time, big-government theorists in the capital city seemed to consider local governments almost as attractive a target as private businesses and other taxpayers.

In effect, Albany treats local government officials—and, by extension, the voters who elect them—as errant stepchildren who can't be trusted to do the right thing.

It's time for New York State to cut costs for, and reduce the red tape on, public schools and municipalities. That means repealing Albany's mandates in areas such as social services, public construction, education, civil service, and management-union relations.

Such reforms would allow localities and school districts to enact major tax cuts for both businesses and homeowners—at least $5 billion, a Public Policy Institute analysis shows. And those tax savings are badly needed. Local taxes in New York are the highest in the nation, by far, and more than double the national average. Those taxes make it harder for businesses to create jobs here, and they drive residents to move away in search of opportunity.

Equally important, **repealing state mandates will improve vital public services, including the schools.** State mandates tie the hands of local officials, impeding almost every effort toward change and improvement.

New York's new generation of political leadership is sympathetic to the problems caused by oppressive state mandates. Governor Pataki and the Legislature have enacted some measures that have cut costs for local taxpayers, mainly in the social services programs that are partly funded by county governments and New York City. Going further with those reforms—in Medicaid's long-term care program, for instance—could reduce social services costs for local taxpayers another $2.3 billion or more.

But the progress has left untouched most of the state mandates that make local government services both more costly and less effective.

And sometimes, state officials seem to think what's needed at the local level is not more freedom to control costs—but more power to raise taxes. A half-dozen bills have been introduced in recent years to permit new local taxes on utility bills, for instance. That approach will make the state's problems worse.

The $163 lightbulb

One of the most frequent complaints from local governments relates to the state laws and regulations mandating the wages that government agencies must pay for construction, electrical and other contracting work. Those rules require "prevailing" wages—in effect, union wages—on all such projects, whether the work is performed by union or non-union workers.

Local officials are virtually unanimous in complaining that the law drives up the cost of projects, both big and small, far beyond what taxpayers should have to pay.

During 1998 and 1999, The Public Policy Institute convened a series of forums with local officials and business leaders, in a dozen communities around the state.

In one of those meetings, the engineering director for a small city told of having to pay a contractor $163 for replacing a bulb in a traffic light. Cost of the bulb: $2.24.

Rather than keep city employees on the clock every hour of every day throughout the year, the city contracts with private electricians to be available for emergency repairs. On other occasions, the city has paid $158, and $147, for replacement of a bulb.

Outrageous? Certainly. Unusual? Not in New York's mandate-driven system of government.

In fact, rather than change the prevailing-wage laws to reduce costs for taxpayers at the local level, many legislators in Albany are endeavoring to make the problem worse. No fewer than 70 members of the Assembly filed bills during the 1999 session that would make the state's prevailing-wage laws more complex for government managers, and more costly for taxpayers.

Another construction-related mandate is the Wicks Law, which requires multiple contractors on most public projects. Together, the Wicks Law and the prevailing-wage mandate drive up construction costs for local taxpayers by at least $1 billion a year.

Our schools and other services suffer

The dollar cost of state mandates is huge. But that's not the only damage they cause—and perhaps not even the most important. Worse, in many ways, is that mandates from the state Capitol make it more difficult for local elected officials and workers to provide vitally needed public services.

And nowhere is that damage greater—nor more troubling—than in the public schools.

It's more important than ever, of course, that teachers and principals be highly-qualified, and focused on excellence. New York's public schools fail to give tens of thousands of children the quality education they need; Education Commissioner Richard Mills and the Board of Regents are insisting on higher standards and more accountability for results. As in every profession, some teachers and principals are incompetent and should be replaced. But reactionary state laws force school districts to go through years of hearings and legal red tape (the case of one principal in Westchester County dragged on for six years!) before attempts to remove poorly-performing individuals are decided. And other statutes, such as the Triborough Amendment to the Taylor Law that governs public employment relations, force school districts to use their limited resources in ways that might not be the best for educational quality.

New York's century-old civil service system is another obstacle to optimal public services. Civil service laws make it harder for public managers to hire the best man or woman for the job—although the Pataki administration has begun to change that. The laws also make it harder to *remove* employees who are not up to the job.

Other mandates hurt vital services. For example, city fire departments around the state must scramble to make up the loss of firefighters who retire early because of a too-broad definition of "work-related" disabilities. And volunteer fire companies and ambulance corps around the state report severe problems recruiting new members, in large part because of new training mandates that go far beyond the level considered necessary just a few years ago.

A good-government agenda for reform

Nothing is more important to New Yorkers than making sure that the public schools do a good job of educating children, and that other vital public services work well. And nothing is more important to New York's economy than continuing to reduce the state's still-high tax burden—in which the biggest problem now is local taxes.

Governor Pataki, the Senate and the Assembly can improve services *and* cut costs for taxpayers—by bringing about real mandate reform now.

Such an agenda could include:

- Enacting real cost savings in Medicaid and other social services;

- Giving school leaders the ability to make sure teachers and other employees are capable and committed to excellence;

- Allowing municipalities and school districts to use the less expensive, more effective procedures that private businesses and individuals use for construction and other contracting;

- Reforming the counter-productive laws that tell public managers how they must deal with public employees; and

- Rewriting liability laws to discourage lawsuits that simply seek "deep pockets" to provide large awards.

Local elected officials sometimes are so discouraged about the prospect for real mandate relief that they don't even bother raising the issue. The county executive and county Board of Legislators in one of the state's largest counties sent the region's state lawmakers a 44-page report on priority requests for the 1999 session in Albany. Not one of the proposals would reduce costs to taxpayers (although some would shift costs from local taxes to state-level taxes). And the city official who had to pay for the $163 lightbulb mentioned earlier was reluctant to have his city identified, partly because of a potential backlash from union leaders.

Of course, mandates aren't the entire explanation for high local taxes. Leaders of municipalities and school districts make decisions on their own that drive up spending and taxes. That's part of the reason tax burdens vary dramatically from county to county, and from one school district to another, even though mandates apply everywhere. Just as state leaders must act to bring down the cost of mandates, local officials must do more to reduce costs on their own. And taxpayers, including business groups around the state, must constantly remind local officials of the need to do that.

County, municipal and school leaders who complain about the high cost of mandates say they could reduce costs for taxpayers dramatically if Albany would ease the mandate burden. The state of New York should give local officials the chance to show they mean business.

New York jobs, particularly Upstate, depend on reducing the mandate burden

The mandate issue is complex and hard for most taxpayers to understand, let alone care much about. But solving this problem is the single most important thing Governor Pataki and the Legislature could do to reduce the sky-high cost of government and improve New York's economy—particularly the Upstate economy.

Upstate, the economic burden of taxes imposed by local government and schools rose sharply from 1988 to the mid-1990s, according to research by Governor Pataki's Office of Economic Affairs. In 1988, property and other local taxes totaled 5.5 percent of Upstate's gross state product (the total of all goods and services produced). By 1996, that figure had risen to 6.8 percent—an increase of nearly one-quarter. (The burden of state taxes has shrunk from 6.1 percent to 5.3 percent of Upstate's total economic output, according to the Office of Economic Affairs.)

"These local tax increases, in the face of a weakening economy, were a contributor to the poor performance of upstate during and after the national recession," Dr. Stephen Kagann, the Governor's Chief Economist, wrote. "In part, excessive local government spending is a consequence of state activity, particularly mandates."[1]

The Office of Economic Affairs estimates that, other things being equal, a reduction of $1 billion in Upstate's tax burden is likely to result in 45,000 additional jobs. Using that estimate, enacting mandate relief sufficient to reduce local taxes by $5 billion would generate an additional 225,000 jobs across the state.

---

[1] *Cutting Taxes, Creating Jobs: The Decline and Revival of Upstate New York*, May 1999.

Two choices: Make New Yorkers keep paying, or change the status quo

"It's easy for people in Albany to say they've cut taxes, but then they impose taxes at the local level" through mandates, a local official in Westchester County said during one of The Public Policy Institute's regional forums.

The understanding that state mandates drive up local taxes, and make it harder to provide quality public services, is nothing new. In 1985, a Syracuse University expert said mandates "are pervasive in New York"—and added that they arise not as good public policy, but as "the line of least resistance for legislators... to reward the groups leaning on them heavily."[2]

That pressure helps explain the lack of action for more than a decade, while criticism of Albany's mandates has grown. For every mandate, there is a special-interest group that opposes reform—Medicaid providers and public-employee unions, to name just two. Former Governor Cuomo proposed some steps to reduce the mandate burden, with little success in the Legislature. Governor Pataki has won some reform of the state's welfare and Medicaid programs, reducing costs for county governments and New York City, while other proposals such as reforming the Wicks Law have not been enacted. The 1999 legislative session came and went with no major mandate-relief action in Albany.

"The days of rhetoric must end," Governor Pataki said at the start of the 1999 session, in announcing a package of mandate-relief proposals. For the sake of taxpayers and those who depend on quality public services, that's exactly right.

How To Cut $5 Billion From New Yorkers' Local Taxes

With reasonable reforms in this area. . .	We could save this much (or more):
Medicaid, welfare and other social services	$2.3 billion
School administration	$150 million
Public construction	$1 billion
Public employee relations	$1 billion
Liability/emergency services/misc.	$800 million

[2] Jeffrey Stonecash, "State-Local Relations: The City and Upstate," in *New York State Today: Politics, Government, Public Policy;* Peter W. Colby, ed.; State University of New York Press.

Chapter 1

Social Services:
A Bit of Progress,
But Taxpayers Deserve
Much More

County governments across New York State collected some $3.4 billion in property taxes in 1999. Outside New York City, counties account for about 1 in every 5 property tax dollars you pay—the rest going to school districts and municipalities.

> With real reform of New York's overwhelmingly expensive social services mandates, county property taxes could be cut by two-thirds, or even further—savings of $2.3 billion that would give the average homeowner and business property owner an overall property tax reduction of more than 13 percent.

The sensible reforms that are needed would have the same cost-saving impact on New York City. With a different tax structure than other areas of the state, city leaders could choose dramatic reductions in income, property or other taxes. (An advisory committee named by Mayor Rudolph W. Giuliani recently recommended $2 billion of tax cuts to be enacted over the coming 10 years, to improve the city's competitiveness.)

And "sensible reforms" does not mean slash-and-burn dismantling of taxpayer-funded medical care, as the pro-spending establishment says whenever any cost savings are proposed. Cutting county property taxes by two-thirds and taking the entire savings from Medicaid and welfare programs would require reducing New York's overall, local cost of social services from 286 percent above the national average to 186 percent above average.[3] Even if the new cost reductions generated similar savings for the state government's share of the program, combined state and local social services expenditures would also still be the highest in the country.[4]

These high social services costs are a direct threat to New York's ability to compete economically. A stark illustration of that came in a 1994 study of state-mandated costs in Monroe County.

The study, by the Center for Governmental Research, compared social services costs in the county (the city of Rochester and its environs) with those in similar counties in other states. The other counties were centered around Charlotte, North Carolina; Columbus, Ohio; Portland, Oregon; Pittsburgh; and Milwaukee. Each of those areas competes directly with Monroe County and other regions of New York for businesses, jobs and residents.[5]

The study's main finding: If Monroe County could reduce social-services costs to the average of its competitor locations, it could cut its general revenue (taxes plus certain other revenues) by 35 percent. Clearly, that could make a big difference in the competition for jobs.

Erie County's Division of Budget, Management & Finance recently conducted a similar analysis. If the county's Medicaid costs were equivalent to those of similar counties in other states, Erie County's property tax levy could be reduced by 45 to 55 percent, the study found.

---

[3] The $2.3 billion savings would reduce local-government costs for social services—the nation's highest, by far—from $8.7 billion to $6.4 billion, or from $479 to $355 per capita. Even with such savings (26 percent of current costs), New York's per-capita local government costs for Medicaid and welfare would still be higher than No. 2 California.

[4] In FY 1996, New York's state and local governments spent just over $25 billion on Medicaid, welfare and related programs, according to Census data; $8.7 billion of that was spent by local governments. Per-capita expenditures were $1,377. Cutting state and local expenditures by $1.7 billion each (the amount needed to reduce county property taxes by half) would reduce total expenditures to $23.3 billion, for a new, per-capita cost of $1,187. Alaska, which ranked second to New York in social services spending per capita in 1996, spent $1,027 per person.

[5] *The High Cost of New York State Mandates: Impacts on Monroe County Taxpayers*, October 1994.

"The level of local property taxes we are forced to levy because of state mandates and cost shifting… is a major reason why upstate job growth has not kept pace with the recent national economic expansion," County Executive Dennis Gorski said.

Livingston County officials, like those in many other counties, calculate costs for mandated services as a proportion of the county property tax levy. Social services costs total nearly 80 percent of the levy, and other mandates drive the percentage even higher.

Why does Albany burden local governments? Because the cost is so high.

New York State has already made progress in reducing mandated costs on localities in social services—in fact, that's the *only* budget area to have seen noticeable reduction of mandated costs. At the same time, no area cries out for *further* reform more than social services.

The reality about New York's spending on Medicaid, cash assistance to the needy and related services is well known. In 1996, U.S. Census data show, New York's state and local governments led the nation in per-capita spending on "welfare"—the Census Bureau category that includes cash benefits, Medicaid and certain other benefits. Spending in New York averaged $1,377 by every resident. That was 89 percent above the national average, and far above any other state.

Texas and California each have more residents than New York; combined, their population is around 50 million, more than 2½ times this state's. Medicaid spending in those two states, combined, is barely above New York's. California alone, with some 12.3 percent of the nation's population, and 14.5 percent of Medicaid recipients, spends only 10.7 percent of the all-states total on Medicaid. New York has less than 7 percent of the U.S. population, and 9.4 percent of recipients—but spends *15.4 percent* of all Medicaid dollars.

All states assign most of the non-federal share of social services spending to the state government, rather than localities. That's true in New York; of the $1,377 per-capita total cost, we paid an average $898 per person through state tax bills in 1996.

That state-level cost *alone* was more than the combined, state-and-local cost borne by taxpayers in each of 44 other states—aside from New York, only Alaska, Maine, Minnesota and Massachusetts spent more than $898 per capita on social services in the last year for which complete data are available. In other words, if social-services costs were like those in most other states, New York could entirely eliminate the share paid by counties and New York City!

But, in New York, the price paid through state taxes isn't nearly the entire story.

As government in New York State decided, over several decades, to create by far the largest and most expensive social services system in the country, the cost was too great for the state treasury alone. In addition, some legislators feared that local welfare administrators would have no reason to restrain costs if Albany paid all the bills. And so, unlike those in other states, New York's governors and legislators assigned a large chunk of the cost to *local* taxing jurisdictions—counties and New York City. As of 1996, New Yorkers paid an average of $479 per person for social services through local tax bills.

As the table on page 13 shows, that local-government cost is by far the biggest in the nation. It's 38 percent higher than California's, and *more than double the cost in any other state.*

All told, the extra cost to counties and New York City creates an added burden on taxpayers of $6.4 billion, compared to what New Yorkers would pay if the local social services burden were the same as the national average.

That doesn't even count the extra tax dollars paid to Albany. Including both state and local government costs, New York's extra social services burden totals a staggering $11.8 billion.

The burden on local governments exists not because state government is miserly—but because the overall cost is so high that state taxes alone aren't enough to pay for it.

A huge problem—and a great opportunity

The tremendous cost of New York's social services system represents a staggering burden on taxpayers, and on the economy. But as Governor Pataki and the Legislature have recognized, it also represents a vast opportunity for reducing the cost of government.

Local Government Spending Per Capita for Social Services, 1996

Rank	State	Amount	Rank	State	Amount
1	**NEW YORK**	**$479**	27	Tennessee	$21
2	California	346	28	Florida	19
3	Wisconsin	215	29	Louisiana	18
4	Minnesota	214	30	Oregon	17
5	New Jersey	156	31	Kansas	15
6	Colorado	143	32	Wyoming	15
7	Ohio	128	33	Missouri	14
8	Pennsylvania	117	34	Texas	13
9	Arizona	113	35	Massachusetts	13
10	Virginia	104	36	Utah	11
11	New Hampshire	103	37	Alabama	10
12	North Carolina	94	38	Kentucky	10
13	Indiana	75	39	Hawaii	10
14	Connecticut	53	40	Georgia	9
15	North Dakota	53	41	Mississippi	9
16	Michigan	46	42	Maryland	8
17	Iowa	44	43	Rhode Island	7
18	Nevada	43	44	Washington	5
19	Illinois	31	45	Oklahoma	5
20	Nebraska	31	46	South Carolina	3
21	New Mexico	30	47	Arkansas	1
22	Montana	28	48	Delaware	1
23	Alaska	28	49	Vermont	1
24	Idaho	27	50	West Virginia	0
25	Maine	26	**U.S. average**		**$124**
26	South Dakota	23	**NY above average**		**286%**

Source: U.S. Census Bureau data; calculations by The Public Policy Institute

As part of the 1995-96 state budget, the Governor, the Senate and the Assembly enacted a variety of Medicaid and welfare reforms that the Governor's Budget Division said would save local governments $612 million a year, compared to what would have been spent in the absence of any legislated changes. The most important reforms included reductions in Medicaid reimbursement rates for hospitals and other healthcare providers, and increased use of managed care.

Continued growth in certain Medicaid costs, and other factors, diminished the actual year-to-year spending reductions
that localities experienced. The Budget Division calculated in
September 1998 that local governments' spending for Medicaid and welfare in 1995-96 totaled $189 million less than the
previous year. And the progress continued in ensuing years, as
local Medicaid and welfare spending declined by a further $92
million over the two years 1996-97 through 1998-99, the Budget Division estimated.

Drop in welfare rolls shows progress is possible

The state's new approach to the income-support side of welfare has also paid off.

As of 1994, New York's welfare caseload totaled 1.6 million
(the number of individuals was much greater, because many
cases represent families). This year, the caseload fell below
1 million for the first time in years. Every county in the state,
and New York City, has seen dramatic reductions in the number of residents on welfare.

In Schoharie County, for instance, new welfare policies
allowed the county to place 483 individuals in jobs after welfare reform began in 1997. As of mid-1998, the county had
only 12 people who were on public assistance, fully employ-
able but not in a training program.

"I didn't think the number would go this low," Barbara
Watt, a supervisor with the Schoharie County Department of
Social Services, told *The Daily Gazette* of Schenectady. "We
needed to support the clients differently."

Other counties report similar dramatic success. The enormous progress on the welfare front, and the Medicaid reforms
that have saved localities hundreds of millions of dollars, are
evidence that Albany can relieve the mandate burden. All
that's needed is the political will.

The state Budget Division estimates that local governments' costs for welfare have been cut by $428 million since
1995, due to shrinking caseloads and policy reforms. While
some counties have reduced property taxes since, it does not
appear that all of those dollars have been returned to taxpayers. Data from the Office of the State Comptroller show
that total tax collections for counties and New York City *rose*
more than $2 billion, or 9 percent, from 1995 to 1997 (the latest
year available). Total property tax collections by counties

outside New York City rose $168 million, more than 5 percent, over the two years. During the same time, counties' spending for purposes other than social services rose by nearly $1 billion, or 10.9 percent.

Local governments—like all levels of government—feel pressure to spend any savings or new revenues. New York's counties, and New York City, will share more than $12 billion in payouts from the national tobacco settlement over the next 25 years. To make sure those dollars are used to reduce taxes, the Legislature could require that all, or a majority—say, two-thirds of the total—be devoted to reducing local taxes. After all, the basic premise of the lawsuits filed by New York and other states was that taxpayers had been forced to spend Medicaid and other dollars to care for persons with tobacco-related illnesses. They were suing to get back the taxpayers' money; now that the states have won, they should promptly return the money to the taxpayers.

County officials say they'd like to use the tobacco money to cut taxes, but may not be able to return all the money because of the rising cost of Medicaid. That's another clear argument for real cost-cutting reform: Without it, a giant ripoff of the taxpayers is almost certain. Meanwhile leaders in some other counties, such as Nassau, are proposing to use the windfall to eliminate budget gaps caused by poor financial planning in recent years. It's hard to explain how such a step would fulfill the stated purpose of the tobacco lawsuits.

Localities should also be required to report to taxpayers every year how they are using the tobacco windfall—how much is applied to tax reduction, new spending, and debt reduction.

Cost-shifting isn't the answer

The recent progress in reforming New York's costly social services programs did not continue in the 1999 legislative session—in fact, the session represented a step backward. During the delay over passage of the 1999-2000 fiscal plan, some of the Medicaid cost-saving reforms enacted in 1995 expired. Those provisions were restored in the budget that was ultimately adopted. In the meantime counties and New York City were forced to pay more than $50 million in needless costs. (The state itself incurred additional costs of $84 million at the same time.)

County officials say the 1999-2000 state budget also shifts tens of millions of dollars in social services costs from Albany to localities. Some of those changes may be defensible on policy grounds. For instance, starting in 1994 the state gave counties additional aid as an incentive to enroll Medicaid clients in managed-care health plans. Now that managed care will be required for all clients, the incentive aid has been eliminated. Whatever the merits of particular changes, it's essential for both state leaders and those at the local level to keep in mind the only real solution to the Medicaid problem: *Cut the cost.*

"Despite a number of innovative reforms and cost containment actions, our system remains, by far, the most expensive in the nation," Governor Pataki's Budget Division wrote in briefing materials accompanying the 1999-2000 Executive Budget. "By virtually every measure, our spending exceeds that of every other state, with New York spending nearly as much on Medicaid as California and Texas combined." The Budget Division added:

> **"State Medicaid spending has left our taxpayers with a burden that they simply cannot afford."**

That point is simply beyond argument. And, without action in Albany, the Medicaid burden may become a crisis once again in the next year or two; experts say the days of high annual increases in health-care costs are returning.

What can be done about it?

New York knows how to cut social-services costs. It just needs political will.

A comprehensive exploration of the reasons that Medicaid is so much more costly in New York, and the solutions to the problem, are beyond the scope of this book. Fortunately, that ground is well-plowed. Reports by state leaders such as former Comptroller Edward V. Regan, and by private-sector groups such as the Citizens Budget Commission, show clearly where costs are out of control.

"The vast majority of social welfare expenditures do not directly aid the poor," CBC pointed out in a 1996 report. "Less than 15 percent of all such spending is for cash benefits placed in the hands of indigent New Yorkers." Most of the money goes to providers of services such as hospitals, doctors, nursing homes and home care agencies. "Thus, huge, productivity-based savings can be realized without harming the neediest New Yorkers," the New York City-based organization said.[6]

The CBC study pointed to another key, but usually ignored, truth about social services spending in New York: "High spending in New York is not due to the state having an unusually large number of poor residents." In 1996, New York's state and local social services spending for every person considered "in poverty" was $8,175—fully 77 percent higher than the average of other states. To put it another way, even though the state ranked only 10th among the 50 states in the proportion of residents in poverty, its Medicaid and welfare spending was the highest in the nation by far.

Clearly, then, trimming out-of-control social services spending—at both the local and state levels—does not require harming the needy.

In fact, one place to start cutting those costs is in bureaucracy. Observers have pointed out for years that the cost of administering programs for the poor is much higher in New York than elsewhere.[7]

In 1996, the combined cost for New York's state and local government administration of welfare, Medicaid, food stamps and other services was more than $2 billion, according to what was then the state Department of Social Services. That was more than was spent on all social services *programs*, in more than 20 of the 50 states! Nearly $1.5 billion of New York's total was local governments' cost (and more than $940 million of *that*, in turn, represented costs in New York City).[8] Those figures represent a stunning amount of taxpayer resources that do not directly help poor people—and they were *down* from previous years. In 1995, the statewide total for administrative overhead was $2.4 billion.

As of 1996, New York spent an average of $1,271 in combined state and local dollars to administer each Aid to Families with Dependent Children case, according to federal data. That

---

[6] *Budget 2000 Project: Social Welfare Spending,* December 1996; summary available through the organization's website, **http://tap.epn.org/cbc/**.

[7] See, for instance, The Public Policy Institute's *The 1990 Taxpayers' Guide to the New York State Budget.*

[8] New York State Office of Temporary and Disability Assistance, *Statistical Supplement to the Department of Social Services Annual Report, 1996.*

Local Administrative Costs for Social Services, 1996

County	Administrative Costs	Total Social Services Spending	Administrative Costs as % of Total
Albany	$18,985,552	$319,361,232	5.9%
Allegany	4,225,819	52,783,561	8.0%
Broome	9,749,662	216,952,352	4.5%
Cattaraugus	5,011,011	88,205,189	5.7%
Cayuga	4,466,449	70,881,112	6.3%
Chautauqua	8,522,637	160,645,169	5.3%
Chemung	4,989,816	107,955,890	4.6%
Chenango	2,632,123	46,156,972	5.7%
Clinton	4,556,580	78,954,125	5.8%
Columbia	3,164,211	66,473,303	4.8%
Cortland	3,101,395	48,732,416	6.4%
Delaware	2,277,555	47,140,774	4.8%
Dutchess	11,911,728	209,391,767	5.7%
Erie	54,599,975	1,162,863,926	4.7%
Essex	2,508,305	41,626,789	6.0%
Franklin	3,410,480	55,732,791	6.1%
Fulton	3,467,055	74,099,061	4.7%
Genesee	2,921,201	46,670,574	6.3%
Greene	2,814,771	43,420,907	6.5%
Hamilton	403,748	3,939,084	10.3%
Herkimer	2,820,229	59,931,559	4.7%
Jefferson	5,804,656	106,700,463	5.4%
Lewis	1,543,663	28,395,423	5.4%
Livingston	3,396,032	53,583,839	6.3%
Madison	2,820,325	49,567,758	5.7%
Monroe	32,979,612	931,518,733	3.5%
Montgomery	2,290,782	62,200,343	3.7%
Nassau	38,081,835	1,106,644,785	3.4%
New York City	944,788,589	20,633,155,684	4.6%
Niagara	14,049,721	215,907,893	6.5%

Local Administrative Costs for Social Services, 1996

County	Administrative Costs	Total Social Services Spending	Administrative Costs as % of Total
Oneida	$14,817,815	$268,291,433	5.5%
Onondaga	29,147,287	534,048,799	5.5%
Ontario	5,079,389	74,624,381	6.8%
Orange	14,605,288	311,421,087	4.7%
Orleans	1,893,880	39,255,171	4.8%
Oswego	6,591,050	115,057,240	5.7%
Otsego	2,591,794	50,785,144	5.1%
Putnam	2,729,271	44,447,019	6.1%
Rensselaer	5,709,682	159,257,148	3.6%
Rockland	15,896,659	274,356,066	5.8%
St. Lawrence	7,243,171	116,098,038	6.2%
Saratoga	4,095,802	110,266,543	3.7%
Schenectady	6,729,998	174,144,757	3.9%
Schoharie	1,981,528	27,292,776	7.3%
Schuyler	1,073,887	19,073,916	5.6%
Seneca	1,784,253	28,560,710	6.2%
Steuben	4,943,692	96,385,824	5.1%
Suffolk	68,297,468	1,175,824,042	5.8%
Sullivan	4,474,581	106,142,298	4.2%
Tioga	3,192,251	39,007,641	8.2%
Tompkins	4,676,387	61,749,184	7.6%
Ulster	7,755,559	183,937,489	4.2%
Warren	2,716,690	51,496,175	5.3%
Washington	2,998,267	56,175,019	5.3%
Wayne	3,782,109	75,440,911	5.0%
Westchester	62,942,010	1,051,415,343	6.0%
Wyoming	2,173,198	30,525,010	7.1%
Yates	929,688	19,665,613	4.7%

Source: N.Y.S. Office of Temporary and Disability Assistance, Statistical Supplement to the Department of Social Services Annual Report 1996

was 95 percent higher than the national average, and more than twice as high as administrative costs in California, Connecticut, Florida, Illinois, Ohio, North Carolina and numerous other states.[9] And that's just the cash welfare program (now known as Temporary Assistance for Needy Families).

Former Comptroller Regan estimated in 1992 that duplicative state and local administration of Medicaid *alone* costs New York taxpayers anywhere from $400 million to $1.9 billion a year; that figure has likely grown along with overall social services expenditures since.[10] Using the low end of the 1992 estimate, allowing for cost increases since, and devoting administrative savings to localities, the right changes at the state and local levels could allow localities to save roughly a half-billion dollars every year by cutting bureaucratic waste in Medicaid.

The Citizens Budget Commission's study also identified a huge potential for administrative savings. It estimated that streamlining administration of New York's public assistance and Medicaid programs could save taxpayers $328 million a year, with no change in benefits. Administrative reforms in child support and foster care could generate further savings, for a total of more than $500 million, the organization said.

Keeping all that bureaucracy is no longer an option

If the need to achieve savings now is not argument enough to cut the cost of administering social services programs, here's another reason: the federal government may force New York to do so. All the states will collect substantial new revenue from the national tobacco settlement (New York's share is some $25 billion) over the coming 25 years. There are rumblings in Congress that the new windfall for states provides a perfect excuse to cut federal aid to state governments. One prime target, according to the authoritative *State Policy Reports* newsletter, is Medicaid administrative funding.[11]

How, exactly, to reduce administrative costs? The experts in the field—public managers in both state and local government—

---

[9] *CQ's State Fact Finder 1999: Rankings Across America*, Congressional Quarterly Inc., Washington D.C.

[10] Office of the State Comptroller, Division of Management Audit, *Staff Study of Trends in Medicaid Program Costs at Local Social Services Districts*, August 1992.

[11] "Uncertain Outlook for Federal Aid," *State Policy Reports*, Vol. 17, Issue 7, September 1999.

should be charged with figuring that out. Clearly, one answer is to cut sharply both (a) the number of bureaucrats who work for the state creating work for localities, and (b) the number of those in county and New York City governments who are needed to respond to Albany's oversight.

A takeover of social services administration by state government would allow counties and New York City to eliminate the second level of bureaucracy that manages Medicaid, welfare and other social services around the state. There is no particular need for 57 social services commissioners, each supervising large staffs. Administrators are needed in the community, of course, but they do not have to be local government employees. The Unemployment Insurance and related operations of the state Labor Department function well on a regional level; there's no reason the same could not be true of the social services bureaucracy. The centralized data banks and other computer systems that would be required for such a change are already largely in place, and are not used to their full potential because of the state-local split in administration.

Centralizing administration could also produce significant program savings. For instance, as the Citizens Budget Commission points out, such a step would make it easier to recover payments from the estates of long-term care recipients.

Just as it's clear that New York can save dramatically on administrative costs, it's equally clear that reforming social services *programs* will pay off even more.

By far the biggest chunk of overall social welfare spending in the state is Medicaid. In 1996, Medicaid represented $21.4 billion, or 61 percent, of the $35.4 billion spent on social services programs statewide.[12]

Medicaid itself can be thought of as two distinct programs. One is health care for the poor. The other is taxpayer financing for long-term care—originally intended for low-income individuals, but now increasingly used by middle- and upper-income New Yorkers as well.

Governor Pataki and the Legislature have begun to bring the health-care side of Medicaid under control, by requiring all recipients other than those in long-term care to enter managed care programs. But there's much more to be done.

---

[12] New York State Office of Temporary and Disability Assistance, *Statistical Supplement to the Department of Social Services Annual Report, 1996.*

Graduate Medical Education Payments By Medicaid, Millions of Dollars, FY 1998

Rank	State	Amount	Rank	State	Amount
1	**NEW YORK**	**$812.0**	27	Alabama	$10.0
2	Michigan	191.0	28	Kansas	9.6
3	Ohio	144.6	29	Oregon	8.6
4	California	129.1	30	Nevada	8.4
5	North Carolina	102.5	31	Colorado	8.0
6	Florida	75.1	32	Connecticut	7.5
7	Georgia	70.0	33	Arkansas	5.7
8	Pennsylvania	66.6	34	Rhode Island	5.1
9	Washington	63.5	35	Nebraska	5.0
10	Kentucky	62.1	36	Utah	5.0
11	Minnesota	58.0	37	New Mexico	4.4
12	South Carolina	57.8	38	Hawaii	2.7
13	Maryland	54.8	39	West Virginia	2.7
14	Louisiana	50.0	40	Maine	2.4
15	Tennessee	46.3	41	New Hampshire	2.1
16	Iowa	43.8	42	Delaware	1.3
17	New Jersey	43.4	43	North Dakota	0.9
18	Texas	40.0	44	Vermont	0.6
19	Wisconsin	37.0	45	Wyoming	0.6
20	Missouri	26.7	46	Alaska	0
21	Massachusetts	25.0	47	Idaho	0
22	Arizona	17.8	48	Illinois	0
23	Virginia	16.1	49	Montana	0
24	Oklahoma	15.7	50	South Dakota	0
25	Mississippi	15.6	**U.S. total**		**$2,370**
26	Indiana	15.0	**NY as % of U.S. total**		**34.3%**

Source: *National Conference of State Legislatures.*

An important first step would be to eliminate the $1.4 billion in "temporary" health-care taxes imposed on both Medicaid and private payors for graduate medical education in the state. Of all the doctors who benefit from these taxes on New Yorkers, about half leave the state to practice elsewhere. The Medicaid program bears more than $800 million of the total cost, by far the highest in the nation; half of that is paid by counties and New York City. (The cost of graduate medical education for New York's Medicaid program is fully one-third of the national total, and more than four times the cost in the second-highest state, Michigan, as shown in the table on page 22.)

Another major improvement would be to reduce provider reimbursement rates for both hospitals and nursing homes, as Governor Pataki proposed in 1999. The Legislature rejected the proposal, and Medicaid costs continued to climb. But a glance at any other state's spending on institutions shows that New York is generous to the point of foolishness. Restructuring provider reimbursements to a more realistic level could generate at least $1 billion in total savings, with half of that going to localities and half to reduce state taxes.

No progress yet on long-term care

Medicaid's financing of nursing home and other long-term care has been little affected by recent reforms. To bring long-term care costs under control, CBC recommended a number of steps including extending managed care to long-term care (nursing homes and home care); and requiring well-off families and individuals to bear more of the cost of long-term care before asking taxpayers to take over the burden.

"New York, more than most other states, has permitted Medicaid to fund middle-class families as well as the indigent," CBC said. "A more equitable approach is to require non-indigent clients and their families to assume more responsibility for financing long-term care." For instance, the state already limits Medicaid funding for nursing home care if a potential recipient has transferred substantial assets to a family member within three years of applying for Medicaid coverage. That time limit does not, however, apply to asset transfers made by applicants for home care. (Home care is used by a far greater proportion of Medicaid recipients in New York than in other states; the difference in self-funding requirements may be one reason.) Applying such a fair and sensible rule to home care would save tens of millions of dollars.

With some such reforms, CBC noted, "The greatest impact of asset limitations would be on the heirs of clients, whose inheritances would be reduced." That's too bad for the heirs—but more fair than the burden Medicaid now imposes on all New York taxpayers, including those of limited means.

The Center for Governmental Research, based in Rochester, came to similar conclusions, in a February 1995 report prepared with the New York State Association of Counties.

"The explosive growth of the cost of long-term care in New York has been attributed to relatively liberal asset transfer rules, particularly for home care," the CGR-NYSAC study said.

The CGR-NYSAC report echoed the Citizens Budget Commission in observing that current Medicaid rules benefit many who are wealthier than the average taxpayer contributing to public coffers.

"The wealthiest group of retirees in United States history are paying remarkably little of the costs of their own long-term care," the CGR-NYSAC study said.[13]

While providing a stick, by requiring families to pay a more fair share of long-term care costs, Albany could also create a carrot in the form of additional tax credits for purchase of long-term care insurance.[14] The state has begun to encourage such insurance; more work is needed.

Reformers suggest these other steps to reduce the overwhelming cost of Medicaid's long-term care:

- **Eliminate first-dollar coverage.** "Medicaid eligibility for long-term care could be provided as a publicly funded insurance policy with a substantial deductible," CGR-NYSAC said.

- **Tighten controls over estate planning methods that are aimed at making the taxpayers relieve middle- and upper-income families.** For instance, current regulations allow relatives to be credited with 50 percent of the balance of a joint bank account, which often represents the savings of an aging loved one. Taxpayers pick up the bill for care, while the family member profits, "even though most or all of the money in the account was initially and exclusively the saving of the applicant," the study said.

- **Create financial incentives for agencies that approve levels of home care.** Suffolk County decided several years ago to institute tighter controls on personal care,

---

[13] *Medicaid Cost Containment: Options for New York,* February 1995.

[14] The tax credit for long-term care insurance was proposed in *Privatization for New York: Competing for a Better Future,* a 1992 report of the state Senate Advisory Commission on Privatization.

and reduced the cost by 27 percent at a time when such costs were rising in most other counties.

- **Create competition for health-care providers.** Ideas include encouraging for-profit hospitals (which bring availability of capital, and lower operating costs) to operate in New York State.

A reasonable initial goal for savings in long-term care is another $2 billion—again, with savings split between state government and the localities. That would still leave New York's long-term care program among the most generous in the nation; it would leave room for consideration of further cost-saving reforms to come.

New York's leaders might even consider statewide takeover of the actual cost of Medicaid—*if* the program's costs can be brought down to the level of competitor states. Virtually the entire savings from cutting the cost would go to the property tax (assuming of course that localities passed the savings on to the taxpayer). In the absence of major program reform, obviously, shifting costs to the state level would leave taxpayers with the same bill they pay now.

Reforming Medicaid will not be easy. The health-care lobby in Albany is well-funded, and it's simple to portray cost-saving reforms as mean-spirited and hard-hearted attacks on Mom and Grandma.

Such reforms could be accompanied by laws that require counties and New York City to direct every dollar of savings to tax cuts—for two reasons.

First, everyone knows that local taxes in New York are too high, and a real commitment to cutting them could help create the political support needed to bring about real change. Second, reducing local taxes sharply would pay off in thousands of new jobs. The economic benefits would likely be most dramatic in upstate New York, which continues to lag the rest of the nation.

Maybe we need another recession

The hospital lobby and other Medicaid providers were able to block Governor Pataki's proposed cost-saving reforms in 1999, partly because of the state's strong financial position. How can the state justify cost-cutting, they argued, when the budget is in surplus?

That argument ignores the ever-present fiscal clouds on the state's horizon. Comptroller H. Carl McCall estimates the state faces potential budget gaps of $2.8 billion in the coming fiscal year and $4.6 billion in 2001-02. Reforming Medicaid would solve two big problems at once—balancing Albany's budget for the long term, and making big tax cuts possible for counties and New York City.

In 1995, the Legislature did agree to significant cost-saving changes to Medicaid as one effort to close a projected $5 billion budget gap. The obvious import is that Albany is willing to reduce senseless expenditures in times of crisis—but not otherwise. Wouldn't it make much more sense to act *now*, when a strong economy would make the transition much easier?

Chapter 2

What's More Important – The Mandate Lobby, or Education?

"What we need is just common sense."

That's how Bruce Brodsky, a longtime school board member on Long Island, sums up the desire among local school officials for reform of costly and inefficient state mandates. It's a refrain that has become more and more familiar from school boards and superintendents all across the state, as New York's system of public schools starts its third century.

In 1795, the Legislature created grants "for the purpose of encouraging and maintaining schools in the several cities and towns..."[15] The state funding was required to be matched by local dollars, but the entire system was optional. By 1814, the Legislature had created a system for development of school districts everywhere in the state, and one of the first big "mandates" was born: Each town was required to match state aid to pay for the schools. The early laws also created the position of Superintendent of Public Instruction, somewhat analogous to today's Commissioner of Education, with authority to oversee the schools.

For more than a century, the relationship between state policymakers in Albany, and elected school boards and appointed administrators at the local level, continued in a

---

[15] Laws of 1795, Ch. 75; cited in "Development of the Education Law in New York," Frank P. Graves, *McKinney's Consolidated Laws of New York Annotated: Education Law.*

partnership that was occasionally antagonistic, but generally considered beneficial to those who matter most—the students. Today, the Board of Regents and Education Commissioner Richard Mills are insisting on higher standards for students (one example of a *good* mandate from Albany). But school board members and superintendents say some policies adopted in recent decades make it hard for them to give students the high-quality education they need so badly.

The harmful interference from Albany means that the people running the public schools have too little authority to:

- **Allocate the essential resources of money and teachers' time.** While school districts in New York spend far more than those elsewhere, school resources are still finite. Locally elected school boards, and their appointees who run the schools, face daunting restrictions on how they use those dollars. For instance, the Triborough Amendment requires that all salaries and benefits (including periodic salary increments) continue after a union contract has expired. And Albany mandates instruction in non-essential subjects, such as the humane treatment of animals and birds—instruction time that inevitably takes away from math, English and other subjects that are most important.

- **Make sure that teachers and administrators are qualified and committed to good education.** Once an educator has worked for three years and been granted tenure, state Education Law makes it difficult and time-consuming to remove bad teachers and administrators. So difficult, in fact, that such individuals typically remain on the payroll for far too long— sometimes, until they retire.

- **Stay focused on excellence.** The people who manage the public schools must spend inordinate amounts of time litigating. employee grievances, sending reports to Albany, and meeting other bureaucratic requirements that don't help kids learn to read or do math.

For any manager, the main steps to providing high-quality products and services are focusing workers on doing the best job, and applying limited resources of time and money in the most effective way. For the managers who run New York's public schools, laws and rules from Albany frequently get in the way.

Property Taxes Per Capita, 1996

Rank	State	Amount	Rank	State	Amount
1	New Jersey	$1,604	27	Pennsylvania	$721
2	New Hampshire	1,520	28	California	715
3	Connecticut	1,422	29	Ohio	713
4	**NEW YORK**	**$1,279**	30	Arizona	703
5	Rhode Island	1,162	31	Indiana	690
6	Vermont	1,155	32	Georgia	652
7	Alaska	1,121	33	North Dakota	640
8	Maine	1,088	34	Idaho	548
9	Massachusetts	1,063	35	Nevada	548
10	Illinois	1,056	36	South Carolina	528
11	Wisconsin	1,054	37	Hawaii	517
12	Nebraska	956	38	Utah	504
13	Wyoming	905	39	Missouri	488
14	Minnesota	884	40	North Carolina	472
15	Montana	883	41	Mississippi	445
16	Washington	845	42	Tennessee	426
17	Iowa	836	43	Delaware	413
18	Florida	820	44	West Virginia	398
19	Texas	797	45	Kentucky	363
20	Kansas	772	46	Louisiana	312
21	South Dakota	762	47	Oklahoma	307
22	Maryland	748	48	Arkansas	300
23	Colorado	743	49	New Mexico	276
24	Michigan	740	50	Alabama	234
25	Oregon	728	**U.S. average**		**$789**
26	Virginia	726	**NY above average**		**62.1%**

Source: U.S. Census Bureau data; calculations by The Public Policy Institute

"Mandates generate controversy on several fronts, including higher taxpayer costs, lower teacher morale, more social engineering, less parental involvement and control," former New York State Teacher of the Year John Gatto has written. "In all these cases, New York education would be better served with greater control at the local level—from teachers, parents, and taxpayers."[16]

School boards need the freedom to use taxpayer resources effectively

There is plenty of reason to distrust the common argument that what the schools need is more money. Per-pupil spending in New York is already far above the national average, and in many ways this state's results are below par (and U.S. average spending, in turn, is higher than that in many other industrialized nations whose children outperform ours on international exams). But there is also plenty of evidence that, through mandates from Albany, New York State prevents the most effective use of all those dollars.

For instance, salaries and benefits amounted to two-thirds—or $18.7 billion—of the roughly $28 billion that New York public schools spent in the 1996-97 school year, according to the Office of the State Comptroller. And state mandates impose strict rules on school boards in their use of those dollars.

Most harmful of all, many school officials say, is the law that requires terms and conditions of union contracts to stay in effect even after a contract has expired. The provision is known as the Triborough Amendment, because the court case on which it is based involved workers for the state's Triborough Bridge and Tunnel Authority.

In the Stillwater Central School District (Saratoga County), teachers refused to agree to a new contract for six years, starting when their former agreement expired in June 1992. For the entire period—the longest teacher contract impasse in state history—teachers continued to receive annual salary increases averaging 3 percent, along with their full health, pension, vacation, holiday and other benefits.

The expired contract required taxpayers to fund 100 percent of the cost of employee health insurance, contrary to practice

---

[16] *Local Control? Mandates and School Budgets,* Citizens for a Sound Economy Foundation, Washington, D.C.; October, 1995.

among most employers. When the district attempted to negotiate an employee contribution to health premiums, the union balked. All but eight of the 111 union members were at experience levels that guaranteed annual pay increments for each additional year of teaching experience, and continued to enjoy higher salaries each year despite the lack of a new contract. It was not until six years later that enough of the teachers—44 of the 111—were no longer receiving step increases to alter the union's stance and prompt agreement on a new contract, according to the New York State School Boards Association.

The school district effectively had no option other than to bear the entire cost. It could not force the union to negotiate the issue, and the Triborough rule eliminated any incentive the union might have had to do so.

Over the course of the six years, annual health premiums for the benefits that these employees received continuously

Teaching humane treatment of birds

Aside from the mandates that waste taxpayer dollars, there are those that steal precious **time**.

Under the Education Law and other mandates, school districts are required to teach about general elections; preventing child abduction; child development; the humane treatment of animals and birds; patriotism and citizenship; the flag and holidays; alcohol, drugs and tobacco abuse; **enforcement regarding** alcohol, drugs and tobacco; highway safety, traffic regulation and school safety; fire drills and fire inspections; fire and arson prevention; game laws and the safe use of firearms; the conservation of natural resources; the history, meaning and significance of the New York State Constitution; parenting; the arts (including visual arts, music and dance); consumer science; home and career skills; health habits and AIDS prevention; genocide; slavery, the freedom trail and Underground Railroad; the Holocaust; the Irish Potato Famine; the procurement and use of hypodermic syringes; hygiene; child abuse; the use of leisure time; highway safety and pedestrian safety, including bicycle safety; head lice, scabies and other contagious diseases; good nutrition; and first aid.

This is all, of course, in addition to the things that parents and employers believe are most important—math, use of the English language, science and so on. By creating higher standards for all schools and all students, the Regents have made it clear that some subjects are more important than others. But the law still requires time-consuming instruction in these other areas.

rose by $2,300 per employee. Union members collected a total of $2.1 million in salary increases without having to negotiate a new contract.

So what's the problem? If we value teachers, shouldn't we pay them well?

Of course. In fact, teacher salaries in New York average more than $49,000 a year. That's 5th-highest in the nation and 25 percent above the national average.

The question is whether New York should allow school boards to decide the best way to allocate the tax dollars they collect from local property owners and through state aid. In Stillwater, for instance, the school board decided it could no longer afford to pay the entire cost of employee health premiums. That's not surprising; most other school districts require employees to pay part of the premium cost, as do more than 80 percent of employers in the private sector. This cost-sharing helps make employees sensitive to the need to restrain the high cost of health care. Perhaps the district could have used those dollars to hire more teachers, as a means of reducing class sizes; to purchase new textbooks; to provide more enrichment for students who need it; to reduce taxes; or for any number of other purposes. The Triborough amendment mandate from state leaders in Albany took that decision out of the hands of the locally elected school board members.

The Triborough law also effectively locks in employee benefits and work rules. In many cases, such generous contractual provisions were agreed upon years ago, when New York's economy could more easily support a costly public sector. Now, almost everyone recognizes that government costs must be reduced, if the state is to be competitive for new business and jobs. The Triborough rule makes such cost reduction especially difficult.

New York's unique benefit for unions

"New York is unique in its approach to the employer's obligation respecting contractual rights," Albany Law School Professor Mary Helen Moses has pointed out. "Coupled with the broad interpretation afforded it by PERB and the New York courts, this provision (Triborough) has drastically changed the face of public sector negotiations in New York."[17] The

---

[17] "Scope of Bargaining and the Triborough Law: New York's Collective Bargaining Dilemma," *Albany Law Review* 56, No. 1, 1992.

state's Public Employment Relations Board, or PERB, administers the Taylor Law and oversees arbitration of contract disputes between municipalities and school districts, and their unionized employees.

School officials support legislation to repeal the Triborough mandate. That would save taxpayers tens of millions of dollars annually; the School Boards Association says the mandate cost districts a total of more than $50 million in 1998. At the same time, such reform would allow elected school board members in each locality more freedom to allocate dollars where they will do the most to improve classroom learning.

Short of repealing the mandate outright, Professor Moses suggests reforms.

"It appears that the state of the law allows, or even requires, both sides to do more strategizing about the use of impasse procedures than engaging in good faith bargaining to attain closure," she wrote. Legislation that passed both the Senate and Assembly in 1990, but did not become law because it was recalled from Governor Cuomo's desk, would have allowed certain exceptions to the rule of no change in the terms of an expired union contract. PERB could change its definition of the terms "mandatory" and "nonmandatory," which would affect the terms and conditions that would remain in effect after a contract had lapsed, Moses says.

School officials' hands are also tied when it comes to making the best use of state education aid. Only half or so of the assistance Albany sends to local school districts is unrestricted operating aid; the rest is "mandated" to go for special education, transportation, buildings, textbooks and so on. Both Governor Pataki and Comptroller McCall have pointed out that the aid formula encourages districts to spend more than they may need. Changing the formula to more of a block grant approach would provide an important incentive for districts to control costs.

Should kids have good teachers?
Some mandates make other things matter more.

Higher standards are coming to New York's schools. Students will benefit—in particular, those who in past years would have received a diploma without receiving a real education. But students cannot be the only ones held to higher standards.

"Higher standards for students require higher standards for teachers," the Regents' Task Force on Teaching said in a 1998 report. "The importance of good teaching cannot be overstated. Efforts to establish higher learning standards will only work if they are embraced by committed professionals who are ready and willing to help students meet the standards."[18]

Most teachers and administrators, of course, *are* committed professionals who work hard to help children learn. But, as in any profession, there are those who do not make the grade.

"My children attend a highly regarded school, but a few mistakes have been made in granting tenure there. They are a constant, troublesome drain on the administration and deprive the children of the opportunity to experience good teaching," Stuart David of New York City wrote in a letter to the editor of *The New York Times*. His conclusion: "We are moving toward a school system that holds students responsible for their performance. The same should be true of their teachers and principals. The elimination of tenure is the only way to make them accountable."[19]

The task force on teaching recommended several major reforms to New York's teacher preparation and oversight system. Among other things, it said, the system must be one in which:

- "Poorly performing teachers are given opportunities and assistance to improve their teaching, and where unsuccessful, are removed from the classroom in a timely manner."

- "The state of teaching and teacher education is continually reviewed by all stakeholders; needed changes are made in a timely manner."

Most school board members and superintendents in New York State are familiar with horror stories about employees who should be kicked off the payroll, but manage to hang on for extended periods because the state's laws are so tilted toward employee "rights."

In the Sachem Central School District on Long Island, a high-school teacher collected a paycheck for more than a year after he was charged in 1993 with rape and sexual abuse of

---

[18] *Teaching to Higher Standards: New York's Commitment,* July 1988.

[19] September 26, 1999.

one teenaged student, and endangering the welfare of a child for fondling another. *Newsday* reported that the teacher, who was suspended with pay in June 1993, continued to collect salary and full benefits even after his eventual conviction—ending only when he was sentenced to 4-to-12 years in prison, in July 1994.

In May of 1999, an assistant principal at the prestigious Stuyvesant High School in Manhattan was accused by a 14-year-old student of sexual contact. There were more accusations; other students said he would leer at them and make sexually charged remarks (which his lawyer characterized as "third-rate Catskills humor"). He collected full pay and benefits from May until mid-July, when he resigned.

"While police investigations and internal probes are conducted, ne'er-do-well pedagogues file papers—or their nails—in the district office. And they get their full salary," the *Daily News* complained in an editorial on the matter.[20]

The high cost of tenure

Of course, most situations when school districts decide an individual teacher or administrator must leave are not as outrageous as the Sachem and Stuyvesant High cases. Even in more mundane situations, though, taxpayers—and students—lose out. Among other things, the law encourages drawn-out disciplinary hearings—and long delays discourage school boards and administrators from bringing charges at all. Disciplinary cases against tenured school employees take an average of 319 days to complete and cost taxpayers $94,527, a survey by the School Boards Association found. That means fewer dollars spent on teaching children to read, repairing school buildings, or reducing school taxes.

Teachers and administrators who are wrongly accused of misdoing can suffer under the delays built into the system, too.

In 1993, the Hendrick Hudson School District in Westchester County filed disciplinary charges against an elementary school principal. The complaints alleged misconduct and insubordination on grounds that the principal wrongly discouraged five children from receiving special education, tutoring and other services. The case dragged on, through 64

---

[20] "Bad Apple," July 26, 1999.

hearings over six years and a total of nearly $1 million in legal fees, before the two sides settled in mid-1999. The school district agreed to pay the principal $600,000 and drop all charges, according to *The New York Times*.[21] The tortuously long hearing system forced the principal to live and work for six years under a professional cloud. Worse, students were consigned to a school whose leadership seemed permanently in limbo. (Indeed, for some students it was permanent—all 325 students enrolled when the case was filed had graduated by the time it was resolved.)

The cumbersome process of disciplining school teachers and administrators is established by the state Education Law. Teachers hired for the first time by a public school district in New York are on probation for three years; at any time they can be dismissed by the school board (on the recommendation of the superintendent). At the end of the three years, the superintendent recommends whether each teacher should receive tenure. The board may choose to grant tenure for each recommended teacher, or reject it.[22] Section 2509 of the Education Law says tenured teachers "shall hold their respective positions during good behavior and efficient and competent service, and shall not be removable except for cause after a hearing." Such hearings and related procedures are governed by Section 3020-a of the Education Law.

Under Section 3020-a, a tenured employee can be suspended upon filing of charges, but generally must continue to be paid until final disposition of the charges. School districts can suspend tenured employees without pay only if the employee has pled guilty to or been convicted of a felony crime involving illegal drugs, or a felony crime involving physical or sexual abuse of a minor or student. (In other words, being arrested and charged with another kind of felony—which could be serious enough to warrant spending years in jail—is not enough to justify suspension without pay.)

As with any rules governing charges of employee incompetence or misbehavior, Section 3020-a attempts to strike a balance between preserving the rights of the employee and

---

[21] June 24, 1999.

[22] One of the many ways that state law bends over backward to protect school employees: If the school board votes to reject tenure that a superintendent has recommended for any teacher, the board must reconsider the issue at a second meeting.

protecting the interests of the employer. But school officials say the law tilts so far in favor of employee rights that students and taxpayers suffer.

Tenure 'reform': Better, or worse?

In 1994, Governor Cuomo and the Legislature enacted changes to Section 3020-a that were intended to make the disciplinary process more efficient. The reforms included requiring a single hearing officer, instead of three-member panels, in most cases; and creating more stringent deadlines. Teachers were granted the right to be told what penalty a school board would seek if charges were upheld, and hearing officers' choices of action were expanded to include requiring remedial action by the employee.

The changes helped, according to the School Boards Association's surveys—before the new law, the average case took 475 days and cost $149,000! Still, there is no denying that the "reformed" 3020-a process works too slowly to adequately protect students and taxpayers from the relatively few school employees who don't belong on the payroll.

In fact, in some key ways the 1994 changes made it harder for school districts to fire incompetent administrators and teachers. Under the old law, for instance, school boards could appeal a hearing officer's decision to the courts if it could be shown that the decision was not supported by substantial evidence, or that the arbitrator had abused his or her discretion. Under the new law, such appeals can only be made under much more rare circumstances—such as if the decision reflects corruption, fraud or misconduct, or if the hearing officer exceeds statutory authority.[23]

School board members around the state complain that the tenure system makes it impossible for them to do the job for which they are elected—to create the best environment for children to learn.

In 1995, for instance, the Patchogue-Medford School Board adopted a resolution stating: "We demand the freedom to reward our good teachers with economic incentives and continued employment, and we must have the discretion to

---

[23] New York State School Boards Association, "3020-a appeals likely to fail—Standard for overturning cases difficult to meet," *School Board News*, August 23, 1999. (Available through the association's website, *www.nyssba.org*.)

discontinue employment of less-than-adequate teachers."[24] School boards in Mechanicville (Saratoga County), South Country (Dutchess County), Pine Plains (Dutchess County) and others have adopted formal resolutions asking Albany to give them the freedom to demand accountability and performance. And these local leaders are not the only ones making the case for such reform.

"Of all the proposals to improve public education, the most effective would be ending tenure for teachers and principals," former New York City Mayor Ed Koch has written. "Give them three- to five-year employment contracts, renewable if they do a good job. Tenure was created to protect those at universities who teach controversial doctrines. Elementary and high school teachers teach basics: reading, writing and arithmetic. Notwithstanding the teachers union, teacher tenure could be ended if state legislators were willing to stand up on the issue."[25]

And most New Yorkers agree that tenure should be eliminated or reformed. The Quinnipiac College Polling Institute found in 1998 that 58 percent of the state's voters oppose lifetime tenure, with an even higher percentage saying it makes teachers less accountable for good results.

Governor Pataki introduced legislation in 1999 to end tenure for principals, at least, and replace it with three-year, renewable contracts. The proposal would establish annual performance reviews that would be the basis for school boards to decide whether to retain principals and assistant principals.

"Principals who fail our children should not get lifetime job security," Governor Pataki said in announcing the proposal. "We must hold principals accountable to ensure that New York's children get the best education possible."

However, the legislation was not among the issues that the state's leaders discussed publicly before the 1999 session ended, and the Legislature did not act on it before leaving Albany for the year.

How many 'poor performers' are there?

How often does the present system fail to identify poor-performing teachers, administrators and other employees?

---

[24] "School boards wrestle with tenure," *New York School Boards*, New York State School Boards Association, April 3, 1995.

[25] "Ending Tenure is the Surest Way to Better Schools," *Daily News*, May 7, 1999.

There is no way to know for sure. State Education Department figures do show that, from 1995 to 1999, the number of 3020-a cases that New York's school districts filed with the department averaged 184 annually. That number represents less than 1/10th of 1 percent of the more than 200,000 teachers employed in public schools statewide.

That figure is almost certainly far smaller than proper concern for student achievement would indicate. It confirms the argument by the School Boards Association that the current 3020-a process serves only to remove teachers with "gross deficiencies" in their ability to do the job.

A 1997 survey by the American Federation of Teachers, *of the union's own members,* indicated that roughly 5 percent of teachers nationwide are rated "poor" by their peers.[26] That cannot be squared with a system that seeks removal of only 1/10th of 1 percent.

A more detailed study, in a different but analagous workforce, was released earlier this year by the federal Office of Personnel Management. It concluded that 3.7 percent of federal government workers are "poor performers." That conclusion was based on a random survey of supervisors, who were asked to rate employees as "good performer," "okay performer," or "poor performer." The middle category included workers who are "meeting minimum performance objectives." Poor performers were those in whom supervisors "are seriously disappointed" and who were "just not pulling their weight,"[27] terms that might equally describe teachers who should not remain in the classroom.

Of course, there is no way to compare the number of underperforming employees in New York's schools with those in the federal government. (And most school districts—like most employers in the private sector—have ways to deal with unsatisfactory employees short of filing disciplinary charges through the 3020-a process, so the Education Department numbers above do not show the full extent of existing action

---

[26] American Federation of Teachers, *Teacher Quality and Tenure: AFT Teachers' Views*, 1997.

[27] *Poor Performers in Government: A Quest for the True Story*, U.S. Office of Personnel Management, January 1999 (available at *http://www.opm.gov/studies/perform.txt*). In counting poor performers, supervisors were instructed: "These are employees with whom you are seriously disappointed. You have little confidence that they will do their jobs right. You often have to redo their work, or you may have had to severely modify their assignments to give them only work that they can do, which is much less than you would otherwise want them to do. They are just not pulling their weight."

against non-performing teachers.) Still, it seems unlikely that the proportion of "poor performers" would vary wildly from one large group of public employees to another, when both are protected by multiple layers of civil service and union rules. And the Task Force on Teaching itself reported candidly that the current system of evaluating teachers "does not always ensure" that evaluation "happens in a way that improves student learning."

Let's say, for the sake of argument, that the proportion of "poor performers" in New York's public schools is only half that in the federal government. That would indicate a total of nearly 3,900 teachers, administrators and others are "poor performers" and should be replaced, or required to improve significantly, for the good of children. That number is some 3,700 more than the actual number of 3020-a cases filed in a typical year. The OPM study also said that the "poor performers" in federal service had been employed an average of 14 years.

Thus, if school districts were to pursue 3020-a cases against all the teachers who are "poor performers," at the average cost per case of more than $94,000, *the cost could run as high as $350 million*. And the hours that superintendents, principals and others would have to spend testifying and preparing for hearings would leave them even less time to concentrate on boosting student achievement.

The OPM study also found that federal government managers often do not make full use of existing avenues to remove sub-par employees. That, too, is sometimes the case in schools. Eliminating state mandates is not the only step needed to strengthen teacher corps—more vigorous management by school leaders is needed in some cases, too. Teacher unions say school administrators do not make as much use of existing disciplinary processes as they should. Administrators and school boards point out, though, that the 3020-a process stacks the deck against them.

An agenda for reforming tenure, while keeping due process

Governor Pataki, former Mayor Koch and the majority of New Yorkers are right—we owe it to today's children to prevent "lifetime job security" for the relatively few educators who do not meet the high standards we need. The New York State

School Boards Association has called for eliminating tenure and giving teachers and administrators five-year contracts that could be extended on agreement of both the employee and the school district. In addition, Assemblywoman Sandra Galef has introduced legislation to require that teachers and administrators renew their licenses every three years. A certain amount of professional development would be required every three years as a condition of renewal.

The Regents will require each school district and BOCES to establish a plan by September 1, 2000, for annual performance review of teachers. This follows from previous policy decisions by the Board that were suggested in the report of the Task Force on Teaching. That's another valuable step forward; more must be done.

Any tenure reform agenda could also consider:

- **Making the 3020-a process faster.** Especially for cases that are not intended to lead to dismissal, there is no good reason for the hearing process to drag out as it does now. Under the new law passed in 1994, a school board is required to state at the outset the maximum penalty it will seek. For penalties less than dismissal, procedural rules should be streamlined, and deadlines shortened dramatically.

- **Allowing suspension without pay in more cases.** Felony drug- and sex-related cases are not the only ones where suspended employees should not receive full pay.[28] In *every* case where the school district seeks dismissal, suspension without pay should be an option for the employer. In other cases, employees could be given a fair length of time to receive their pay while on suspension. A fair number might be 160 days, the maximum time that hearings are supposed to last. Employees who are suspended without pay, and are ultimately vindicated in the hearing process, could be entitled to collect back pay, with interest. Otherwise, the existing system gives employees and their representatives every incentive to make the hearing process last as long as possible. Non-instructional employees, such as

---

[28] In one case, according to the School Boards Association, the state Court of Appeals ruled that a suspended teacher was entitled to full pay during adjournment of a 3020-a hearing, even though the teacher requested the adjournment because criminal charges arising from the same incident were being resolved.

secretaries, can be suspended without pay for up to 30 days pending determination of charges. Those rules give school districts the ability to protect against incompetence or criminality in less essential areas of school life. Why not the classroom?

In New York City, Mayor Rudolph Giuliani and Schools Chancellor Rudy Crew have both proposed to the union representing school principals that a new labor contract include an end to tenure for principals, along with an unprecedented pay increase of 30 percent. The union at first rejected the idea, saying it would never agree "to give up one ounce of job protection."

The reaction by the principals' union was criticized as an open admission that the unions representing school employees just don't care about improving education for the predominantly minority, often lower-income students that the city's public schools serve. In fact, of course, the principals' union—like those representing other workers in education and the broader marketplace—has a legal responsibility to put the interests of its members first. Public policy makers must keep that in mind when soliciting the unions' opinions on tenure and other issues, and give first consideration to the children. (In the fall of 1999, the Giuliani administration and the principals' union were reportedly close to agreement on new restrictions on tenure, in exchange for large raises.)

Robert R. Kiley, president of the New York City Partnership and Chamber of Commerce, has suggested that one approach to reforming tenure for principals could be to petition the Public Employment Relations Board to designate principals' positions as managerial in nature and thus exempt from collective bargaining.[29] That approach would have a number of advantages. Among other things, it would obviate the need to impose the costs of a 30 percent pay hike on taxpayers in exchange for a few basic and obvious reforms.

School leaders' mistakes don't help

State mandates aren't the only hurdle to more accountable and higher-performing school professionals. Sometimes, school districts themselves give away more authority than they should.

---

[29] "It's Time to End Principal Tenure," *Daily News*, June 21, 1999.

One example is the current contract the New York City schools system negotiated with its teachers' union, the United Federation of Teachers.

"Under the contract, principals don't control who teaches at their school," University of Massachusetts economist Dale Ballou concluded in a widely noticed study sponsored by the Manhattan Institute and issued in 1999. "The contract pushes veteran teachers on them through the seniority-based UFT transfer system and through 'excessing,' transferring teachers in reverse order of seniority from over-staffed schools. There is no guarantee that teachers who transfer in will share the educational views of the principal or other teachers at the school."[30]

The Ballou study shows the interplay between state laws and decisions made at the local level, together creating an atmosphere that is virtually guaranteed to hurt New York City children's prospects for a good education:

> To get rid of a tenured teacher, a principal typically must thoroughly document professional misconduct to support an unsatisfactory rating given out during an annual evaluation. The contract gives teachers the right to see their files and submit grievances over any particular items, with possibilities of appeal to the chancellor's office. The contract even provides for arbitration if the union believes there are contractual grounds for objecting to the chancellor's decision. Any unsatisfactory rating founded on such items can also be appealed to the Board of Education's Office of Appeals and Reviews. If the principal's rating is sustained, to fire the teacher, the superintendent of the teacher's district can then refer the case to the Office of Legal Affairs to bring a legal case—complete with cross-examined witnesses. Even if the Office wins its case, remedial action—such as a leave of absence, continuing education, counseling, or medical treatment—may be ordered instead of firing. The process may not stop there; civil service protections give a fired teacher the right to appeal to the state Supreme Court.

---

[30] *The New York City Teachers' Union Contract: Shackling Principals' Leadership*, June 1999.

From February 1997 to March 1998, Professor Ballou found, the city schools' Office of Legal Affairs "won cases against just 17 teachers—an absurdly small number in a vast system that employs 68,000 teachers."

The state's courts, too, have contributed to the problem. In 1993, the Court of Appeals ruled that school districts must provide 60 days' notice (and therefore 60 days of pay) when dismissing a probationary teacher—even if the time extends beyond the expiration of the probationary period.[31] In the private sector, two weeks' notice is often considered adequate when an employee—particularly one on probation—must be dismissed. For schools, though, six times that amount is required! Every day's pay for a dismissed teacher is a day's pay that does nothing to help students learn.

The mandates that make it difficult for school boards to remove incompetent or misbehaving teachers are especially troubling now that New York State's schools are under increasing pressure to improve educational results.

The Education Department could easily take one useful step toward enhancing performance by teachers and administrators—simply by gauging the quality of preparation and performance of these critically important individuals. The new School Report Cards that Commissioner Mills and the Regents have initiated are already sparking countless conversations, in districts around the state, about how schools can improve. That experience proves something world-class private companies have known for years: What gets measured, gets better.

Indeed, there is already a state law requiring SED to report annually to the Governor and the Legislature on, among other things, "information concerning teacher and administrator preparation, turnover, in-service education *and performance*" (emphasis added). This is the same law, enacted in 1987, that requires the department to report on enrollment trends, student achievement, graduation rates and other key indicators. And the department submits, every year, an informative and clearly presented report on those subjects. Not once, however, has the report included the required information on teachers' and administrators' qualifications and performance. It should.

---

[31] *Tucker v. Board of Education, Community School District No. 10*, 82 N.Y.2nd 273 (1993).

School districts often complain that state mandates make it harder for them to maintain the highest quality teaching corps. That's true—but it's not the whole story, as the Task Force on Teaching pointed out. It said: "The local school district is responsible for evaluating how well teachers perform in the classroom. The present evaluation system, however, does not always ensure this happens in a way that improves student learning."

Wasting time

Beyond the additional costs imposed by mandates such as the Triborough amendment, schools must deal with a host of laws and rules that have nothing to do with seeing that Johnny and Janey can read. Examples include:

- The Holland Patent Central School District was forced to go through a PERB hearing because the school superintendent asked a food-service worker who had filed several union grievances whether she was "happy" with her job. The superintendent said he wanted to understand the workers' complaints better, in hopes of solving them informally. A PERB administrative law judge agreed with the Civil Service Employees Association that the question implied that employees who file grievances "do not fit" in the district—and ruled that the district had engaged in an improper practice under the Taylor Law.

- The Monticello Central School District had to go to court to defend its right to suspend a student who distributed, on school grounds, a publication that encouraged other students to urinate on floors, throw garbage around the school courtyard, write graffiti on school walls and smoke in the bathrooms. The Education Department had ruled that the suspension violated the student's rights to freedom of speech and expression. The Appellate Division of state Supreme Court reversed the department, and the Court of Appeals upheld the lower-court ruling.

- The Riverhead Central School District had to go to PERB to uphold a directive to teachers that they contact any students who were failing their classes, and offer remedial help. The teachers union complained that the requirements must be negotiated first. PERB's administrative law judge upheld the district.

- The state requires school districts' plans for building projects to be reviewed by state-approved architects. The process typically adds tens of thousands of dollars in fees, and several months of delay (often making the difference of a semester or even an entire school year). As school leaders in Westchester County and Long Island asked during The Public Policy Institute's forums, all architects are licensed by the state Education Department before they begin practice—why is another layer of review needed?

All of these things force school districts to devote time and money to administration, rather than the classroom. Barely more than half of all the people who work in or oversee New York's schools are teachers. Data from the U.S. Department of Education show that's a problem in most of the states—but more so in New York. Even including instructional aides, guidance counselors, librarians and school-level administrators, "in-school staff" totals only 63 percent of the total in New York, compared to a national average of 67 percent.[32] (The rest of the jobs are at the school district level, and in county and state government.) That may appear to be a small difference, but matching the national trend would mean thousands of additional teachers working directly with children. Ideally, of course, the great majority of payroll would go into the classroom, in New York and other states alike.

More than ever, New Yorkers are demanding that the schools provide a world-class education. Superintendents, principals and other administrators must play an important role in satisfying that demand. Their time should not be taken up with extraneous issues.

The cost of special education: too high in both dollars and students' lives

New York has traditionally been among the most generous of states when it comes to caring for those with great need. Education of students with special needs is one example. But, as in other areas such as social-services programs, special education has grown to where it is too costly for taxpayers, and harms many of those it was intended to help.

---

[32] "Top-heavy," Forbes, November 2, 1998; p. 60.

The special education system has drawn criticism and calls for reform from observers as varied as Governor Pataki and former Governor Cuomo; New York City Mayor Rudolph Giuliani and City Comptroller Alan Hevesi; and school boards from rural upstate areas, New York City and the metropolitan suburbs.

The biggest problem: Too many kids are labeled as needing special education. Minority children are especially likely to be assigned to the program. In many cases, the children lose out, because they stay outside mainstream education for years and never receive the more challenging education of which they're capable.

Taxpayers suffer as well—special education adds hundreds of millions of dollars to New York's already high school costs. *Newsday* reported that the two directors of a Nassau County preschool program for disabled children each collected more than $150,000 in salaries—more than the highest-paid school superintendent on Long Island.[33]

In a 1994 report, Comptroller Hevesi's office found that the New York City school system spent nearly one-quarter of its budget on special education programs, but did not even have any way of measuring whether disabled children were receiving an education or learning useful skills.

Change is underway. The state Education Department reported in early 1999 "a mixed picture of both improvement and a lack of progress in special education placements." The increase in the rate of special education placements slowed in 1998, the department said. On the other hand, relatively fewer special-ed students were placed in regular classrooms.[34]

The improvements came about in part because of reforms already enacted by the Legislature, according to Education Commissioner Mills. He and the Regents have called for further reforms, including changing financing formulas to eliminate incentives for school districts to assign more students to special education. The primary goal of such reforms would be to improve the prospects of a quality education for as many students as possible. But costs would be reduced, as well, most likely by $100 million a year or more.

---

[33] "Education at Great Expense: Preschool costs soar amid complex rules, lax oversight," November 12, 1997.

[34] "Chancellor Hayden and Commissioner Mills Release 'Mixed Picture' of Special Education Data," press release, February 2, 1999.

Two new programs that cost millions

Over the last decade, state leaders have created—and mandated that counties pay much of the cost of—two new programs for youngsters who have special needs. Both programs fall under the federal Individuals with Disabilities Education Act.

The first, established in state law in the late 1980s, provides preschool special education for 3- and 4-year-old children. County taxpayers pick up 40.5 percent of the cost, with the rest coming from the state. In a system almost guaranteed to drive costs ever higher, the same organizations that provide the services often perform the assessments that lead to children being placed in their programs.

In 1992, Governor Cuomo and the Legislature created the Early Intervention Program for infants and toddlers with disabilities. County taxpayers pay half the cost. As with the program for 3- and 4-year-olds, county officials have only a minority voice regarding early intervention placements, the level of services to be provided, or how the programs are run.

Expenditures for the two programs add up to nearly $1 billion a year, paid by New Yorkers' state and local taxes. In terms of the county share, it's taxation with a little representation—counties are mandated to pay the cost, but do not control how the programs operate.

One way to control those costs would be to reduce the control that provider organizations have over assessments and placements. Another would be to require that providers be selected based mainly on how successful and cost-effective their programs are.

Every school a charter school?

"What we should do is make every school a charter school," one school official told The Public Policy Institute during a forum on mandate relief earlier this year. In other words, give every student the benefit of attending a school where what counts is student achievement, rather than following Albany's mandates.

For some time, the education establishment attempted to demonize anyone who called for alternatives like charter schools. But the obvious fact that schools shortchange thousands of students every year—and that those children deserve a chance, just like everyone else—is now the mainstream.

"More and more reformers are saying that schools must be freed, legally, of school bureaucracies' rules and constraints and of unions' veto power," Neal R. Peirce, one of the nation's most respected observers of government, has written. "Only then, they argue, can schools become the truly independent, cohesive teams of motivated, skilled and caring professionals they need to be—for the children's sake."[35]

Those who are building the schools of tomorrow clearly understand the importance of breaking away from the constraints of the past.

"Unfettered by the bureaucratic constraints imposed on the traditional public schools, we will be free to employ the best practices from the worlds of education and business to create a school that aspires to excellence," Aaron R. Dare, president/CEO of the Urban League of Northeastern New York, said of the New Covenant School his organization helped create in 1999 in a poor neighborhood in Albany. "One shudders to think of the number of carefully considered and well-intentioned education reforms that have fallen victim to simple but intractable institutional constraints —stifling rules and regulations, an obstinate and misguided administrator, teachers more concerned with tenure than teaching, and so on.

"And because charter schools are schools of choice, they are directly accountable to parents, who can vote with their feet if they are dissatisfied," Dare added.[36]

Albany's mandates lock into place a system that focuses on institutions and employees, rather than children. Charter schools put the focus back where it belongs—on excellence in education.

The charter-school law that Governor Pataki pushed through in 1998 allows 50 charters issued by the Charter School Institute of the State University of New York, and 50 by the Board of Regents. (An unlimited number of existing schools can convert to charter school status, with approval from parents and the school board.) The law has excited interest across the state, particularly in urban areas where parents ache to find educational opportunities for their children. It appears likely that applications, particularly to SUNY, will snowball in the next year or two. More charter schools

---

[35] "The Gathering School Revolution," *National Journal*, January 4, 1997.

[36] "Charter Schools Offer New Opportunities," *Saratoga Business Journal*, August 1999.

will be needed to provide a place for every student who wants one. Unless, of course, all of the mandates that prevent existing schools from focusing on excellence are repealed. (In the meantime, New York's traditional public schools should be watching the charter schools closely, for inspiration and to learn from their innovation.)

The 500 children attracted to the New Covenant School are mostly from minority, low-income families. They illustrate the reality that the problems in traditional schools hurt these neediest students most of all. Public elementary schools across the state that have high minority populations lag far behind other schools in teaching children to read and achieve other academic success.[37]

Allowing *all* schools the opportunity to achieve at the highest level, by repealing senseless mandates, is the least New York can do for those children.

---

[37] For a detailed discussion of this issue, see *Separate and Unequal: The Reading Gap in New York's Elementary Schools*, The Public Policy Institute, March 1998.

Chapter 3

Reconstructing the Laws on Public Construction

In an era when government seems to provide more services than were imaginable a few decades ago, the basics—things like bricks and mortar, asphalt and concrete, electrical wiring and plumbing—are as important as ever.

Building and maintaining schools, highways, offices, fire stations, bridges, water systems and other capital projects is a $10 billion-plus annual business for governments in New York State. Local governments, including New York City and all the state's school districts, are responsible for some $4 billion of that total.

Ideally, of course, all that contracting work would be done efficiently—at a reasonable cost to taxpayers, with each project completed in a reasonable period of time. But laws imposed by Albany make much of New York's public contracting far from ideal.

As a result, New Yorkers pay more than they should—through both state taxes, and local taxes. And the citizens for whom all those dollars are spent—school children, for instance—suffer needless delay.

Two prime culprits stand out among the various mandates New York's governors and legislators have imposed on contracting work by localities and school districts. Albany's laws and regulations require payment of prevailing wages—in effect, union wages, along with union work rules—on most public contracting projects. That covers not only construction but also electrical and mechanical repair jobs, such as the traffic bulb replacement described in the Introduction. Second, the state's antiquated Wicks Law requires multiple contractors on most construction and building renovation projects, making it impossible for taxpayers to enjoy the cost savings and efficiencies that most private-sector projects realize from use of a general contractor.

> **All told, the prevailing wage, Wicks Law and other mandates drive up construction and related costs for local governments and schools by more than $1 billion a year.**

'Prevailing' wages: New York's law is one of the nation's worst

Of all the costly mandates the Legislature has imposed on localities, one of the most frequently criticized is the law that, in effect, forces local officials to pay union wages for construction projects of any size.

A Federal statute known as the Davis-Bacon Act, adopted in 1931, requires "prevailing wages" to be paid on many federally financed construction projects. New York's law—based partly on a provision inserted in the state Constitution in 1938—imposes similar requirements. Some two-thirds of the other states also have "little Davis-Bacon" laws.

Wherever they exist, such laws are guaranteed to drive up taxpayers' costs for most construction projects. Union wages are almost universally higher, and benefits more generous, than those for non-union construction workers. And union contracts make projects more complicated for public managers—which means *more* additional cost, to say nothing of greater difficulty and more time needed for completion.

"The people have to pay more taxes to get the job done," Millie Wise, supervisor of the small town of Plainfield, Otsego County, said of prevailing-wage rules during The Public Policy Institute's regional forum.

New York State's prevailing-wage statute is notable for the extra costs and difficulty it imposes on taxpayers and construction managers, according to a national study of such state-level laws.

"Amendments through the years and contrary opinions by various attorneys general have made it one of the most turgid and most difficult to abstract," or summarize, according to Armand J. Thieblot, Jr., a former professor at the University of Pennsylvania's Wharton School and now a consultant.[38]

Having studied state and federal prevailing-wage laws for more than 25 years, Thieblot ranks the 31 state laws for severity—using factors such as the types of projects that are exempted, dollar thresholds, and how strongly the law pushes union wages as the effective "prevailing" wages. Massachusetts' law is ranked as the most burdensome in the nation; New York, New Jersey and California are tied for second among the 31 states.

The complexity of New York's law stems in part from the picayune details often found in union contracts regarding job classifications and pay levels. For example, the prevailing wage schedules in some parts of the state list five different wage schedules for laborers—with wage differences as little as 15 cents per hour. Typical school business administrators and town public works directors may have a hard time dealing with such arcane details. And so do many non-union contractors, who simply avoid bidding on taxpayer-funded jobs. In other words, the law not only drives wage levels to union scale, it effectively makes it hard for public managers to hire non-union contractors. (And that, of course, is a major reason organized labor lobbies for prevailing-wage legislation so fiercely.)

The cost of a new library roof

In the Village of Johnson City (near Binghamton), the prevailing-wage mandate came into play when the village library needed a new roof several years ago. The contractor originally estimated the cost at $9,800, Mayor Harry Lewis said. By the time prevailing wages had been factored into the bids, though, the project ended up costing taxpayers more than $20,000.

"The Davis-Bacon requirement to pay 'prevailing wages' among other things reduces the number of projects we can

---

[38] Armand J. Thieblot, Jr., *State Prevailing Wage Laws: An Assessment at the Start of 1995*, published by Associated Builders & Contractors Inc., Rosslyn, Va., January 1995; and *Government Union Review: A Quarterly Journal on Public Sector Labor Relations*; Public Service Research Foundation, Vienna, Va.; 1983.

complete with Community Development funds," says Clara Lou Gould, mayor of the city of Beacon (Dutchess County).

John M. Davis, former Monroe County Director of Engineering, estimated that prevailing wages cost the county $10 million a year. The wage requirements boost labor costs 40 percent, based on information his department obtained from local contractors; 25 percent or more of construction costs are labor; and the county's total construction program costs roughly $100 million a year.

Several years ago, according to Davis, his office sought bids from both private construction companies and from the county's Environmental Services Department for a project at the county landfill. The county employees' bid was just over $7 a ton of solid waste.

"The lowest private-sector bid was $12.95 a ton, or 84 percent higher," Davis said. "The major reason was/is the difference in wage rates."

Besides being complex and hard to understand, New York's prevailing-wage law is stricter and more punitive than those in most other states. For example:

- The federal Davis-Bacon Act exempts projects with estimated value below $2,000 (not a major exclusion, given construction costs—but at least enough to cover changing a lightbulb!). Most of the other states that impose the prevailing-wage mandate provide some exemption. Pennsylvania, for instance, exempts up to $25,000; Connecticut, $50,000 for new construction; Maryland and New Hampshire, $500,000. New York imposes prevailing wage requirements *on every project,* no matter how small.

- The federal and state prevailing-wage rules sometimes differ, and states can decide whether to use wage classifications set by the U.S. Department of Labor or to establish their own rates. More than half of the states that impose prevailing wage choose one or the other consistently. New York, and a few other states, require public managers to choose whichever rules impose *higher* wages (and taxpayer costs) on a given project.

- A number of states—Michigan, Maine and Tennessee among them—specify that prevailing wages are not required on local-government projects, or give localities the option of choosing whether to be covered. Not New York.

- Since 1983, the federal Davis-Bacon Act has applied only when a given wage is indeed "prevailing" in a given community—when the wage is used by a majority of contractors, or is identified through surveys as the actual average wage. Some states, including New York, impose "prevailing" wage when the state Labor Department determines that as few as 30 percent of workers in a given region earn that wage.

The 30 percent rule was enacted by Governor Cuomo and the Legislature in 1983. How does the department know whether 30 percent of carpenters in Utica, for example, earn a given wage? It doesn't. It simply consults the local carpenters' union contract. And in almost every area of the state, union workers are a minority of the total in given specialties—their wages are anything but "prevailing."

New York is different from many other jurisdictions in one other, crucial way: **Other governments are moving away from the costly, cumbersome requirements of prevailing wages.** Nine states have eliminated their prevailing-wage laws in the last two decades. They include Kansas and Arizona, which—like New York—were among the first states to enact such laws. Other states, including Ohio, Connecticut and Delaware, have raised the threshold at which the law applies or made other useful reforms in recent years. While New York has begun to take some steps administratively, more significant reforms that would require legislation are nowhere on the horizon. And, as mentioned in the Introduction, nearly half the members of the Assembly have proposed various bills that would make the problem worse.

As with every needless mandate, prevailing wages hurt those who depend on public services. School boards and municipalities constantly choose among construction plans they'd like to pursue, because high costs do not allow every priority to be met. A new classroom is eliminated here, a new roof delayed there, a new neighborhood police substation around the corner eliminated from consideration.

The poor, and minorities, lose out under prevailing-wage mandates

Often, the prevailing-wage mandate hurts poor and minority New Yorkers the most, as *The New York Times* observed in a

1993 editorial on a bill that would have expanded the prevailing wage law's definition of "public works."

"Prevailing wages mean high union wages, and the definition of public works has been expanded well beyond its usual meaning of schools and bridges to include *private* [emphasis in original] projects, like low-cost housing, that receive tax and other public subsidies," the *Times* commented. Under the proposal which at that point had passed the Senate and was being considered by the Assembly, the cost of renovating an apartment with public funds would have risen from $8,000 to more than $13,000, according to the newspaper.

"The union workers and large contractors who hire them are powerful constituents," the *Times* said. "The poor renters and minority contractors who will be trampled aren't."[39]

As the editorial suggested, prevailing-wage laws tend to hurt minority-owned construction companies, which tend to be relatively small and non-union.

Referring to the federal law, the owner of a minority contracting company in Seattle wrote in *The Wall Street Journal*: "To seek Davis-Bacon contracts, minority firms must not only pay inflated wages and adopt inefficient work practices, but must expose themselves to huge compliance costs and threats of litigation and union harassment...Davis-Bacon remains a principal reason why blacks are unemployed at twice the rate of whites in the construction trade."[40]

The U.S. General Accounting Office, the nonpartisan, investigative arm of Congress, said in a 1979 report that prevailing-wage requirements "discourage nonunion contractors from bidding on federal construction work, thus harming minority and young workers who are more likely to work in the non-unionized sector of the construction industry."[41] And state Comptroller H. Carl McCall, then president of the New York City Board of Education, said in commenting on a 1992 proposal to bring more minority workers into publicly funded contracting jobs that "construction unions have had a longstanding pattern of racial exclusion."[42]

---

[39] "A Bad Bill for the Poor," November 5, 1993.

[40] Nona M. Brazier, "Stop Law That Hurts My Minority Business".

[41] *The Davis-Bacon Act Should Be Repealed*, April 1979. (While some Republican members of Congress are now pushing to repeal Davis-Bacon, both the Senate and House of Representatives were controlled by Democrats at the time of the report.)

[42] Ronald Sullivan, "Unstated Goal of Jobs Plan: Open Unions," *The New York Times*, December 26, 1992.

Even unions see a problem

Sometimes, even unions don't like New York's prevailing-wage law.

In 1992, the Civil Service Employees Association—which represents more than 200,000 workers statewide and is one of the largest members of the New York State AFL-CIO—built a new regional headquarters in Fishkill. At least one of the subcontractors on the job was non-union, and the general contractor told the Middletown <u>Times Herald-Record</u> that his priority in choosing firms was their price and ability to get the job done. Officials of the local building trade unions complained bitterly, and one union contractor told the newspaper: "I wouldn't have wasted my time bidding if I'd known I'd be competing with non-union guys." CSEA's comptroller replied: "It's a question of cost." [43]

Who else gets hurt by prevailing-wage laws? The National Federation of Independent Businesses, the small-business lobbying group, says small contractors in general suffer. Entrepreneurs who may be well qualified to get the job done have little time to spend on the paperwork and payroll analysis that prevailing-wage rules require, and may not have the resources to pay the higher wages required by the law.

The prevailing-wage requirement is not going to disappear entirely, short of an amendment to New York's state Constitution (labor leaders succeeded in having the rule inserted during the 1938 Constitutional Convention). But much can be done to change the meaning of "prevailing," and other important details.

During the Pataki Administration, the state Labor Department has already changed some of the administrative practices that previously amounted to outright contempt for local government managers and the taxpayers they represent. Some municipal officials report, for instance, that the department used to side almost automatically with complainants who alleged that contractors and their municipal clients were violating wage classification or other rules. Now, "they're more fair and not totally one-sided," one local official said.

The Labor Department could do more, under existing law, to ease the burden that prevailing-wage rules impose on localities. Simply issuing written guidelines for public

[43] "CSEA Finds Prevailing Wage Expensive," reprinted in New York State Conference of Mayors, *Municipal Bulletin*, May/June 1992.

works projects would eliminate confusion and delays by contractors; the department has been considering such a step. The department could establish actual wage surveys to determine the "prevailing" wage in a given area, rather than relying on union contracts in every instance. Alternatively, local government associations or other groups could be allowed to perform surveys, subject to review by the department.

Through legislation or action by the Labor Department, Albany should exempt many projects from prevailing-wage requirements. A threshold of $1 million, as Governor Pataki has proposed for the Wicks Law (see below), might be a reasonable first step. Reforms should also include allowing municipalities to enact local laws that are less restrictive than the state prevailing-wage laws and rules; and defining the "locality" in which prevailing wages are found as an actual locality, not the territory covered by a big union contract.

Wicks Law: A tribute to the power of special interests in Albany

While prevailing-wage laws and rules are the dirty little secret of Albany's construction-related mandates, the other major issue in this area is anything but a secret. Good-government groups and respected officials, in both state and local government, have been calling for repeal of the Wicks Law for decades.

A case that occurred in Albany shows why. In July 1999, a state Supreme Court ruling ordered the City School District of Albany to pay a contractor $175,783 for breach of contract. The firm had claimed that the district failed to coordinate numerous contractors working on the city's Public School 23 (the Albany School of Humanities), causing the firm to incur additional costs. The Wicks Law required the school district to retain responsibility for coordinating the work of separate contractors. The school reconstruction ended up with significant cost overruns and delays in completion.

One of the most authoritative studies of the Wicks Law, by the staff of the state Budget Division, concluded in 1987 that eliminating Wicks would reduce the cost of many typical construction projects by 30 percent.[44] Annual statewide savings

---

[44] *Fiscal Implications of the Wicks Law Mandate*, May 1987.

would total $300 million to $400 million, according to the study. That figure would be even higher today, as capital construction spending has risen in the years since.

In 1996, the Citizens Budget Commission calculated that a "conservative" estimate of savings from Wicks repeal would be 10 percent of capital costs. Using that figure, CBC estimated New York City would save $282 million a year in annual debt service from Wicks repeal, and state government $238 million. Including savings for local governments outside New York City, the statewide total for localities would easily surpass $500 million a year.

The Legislature itself has, in essence, formally found that allowing localities to escape the Wicks mandate is good for local taxpayers. The Legislature has exempting buildings erected by the New York City School Construction Authority from the law, and exempted the Niagara Falls School District from competitive bidding and Wicks rules for construction of a new high school.

Most recently, a 1999 study performed for the School Construction Authority found that Wicks-type construction would require some 49 months (more than four years!) to complete a new school. Without the Wicks mandate, the authority plans to use design/build single contracts that should result in construction time of no more than 24 months. The authority's Wicks exemption will save $192 million, according to PricewaterhouseCoopers LLP, the highly regarded consulting firm that conducted the study. Without the exemption, keeping spending at the same level would mean the loss of seven new schools. In other words, eliminating the Wicks mandate means the difference between a shoddy educational environment, and a positive one, for thousands of school children—in addition to savings for taxpayers.

Wicks raises safety concerns, too

The School Construction Authority study found other reasons to eliminate Wicks. For rehabilitation projects, it said, "safety rules in an occupied school would be more difficult to enforce with four prime contractors."[45]

Construction experts have a simple question for those who argue for keeping the Wicks Law intact: If the existing

---

[45] *Impact of the Wicks Law on Public Construction in New York City*, March 1999.

process is so efficient, why do we need a mandate? Surely school districts and municipalities will choose the multiple-contractor process if it saves money.

Governor Pataki has proposed reforming the Wicks Law by raising the floor for exemption, from the current $50,000 to $2 million for most localities, $5 million for most large municipalities and $10 million for New York City. That would reduce costs for taxpayers noticeably.

As the state Association of Towns has pointed out, though, those new thresholds would leave much public construction still burdened by the Wicks mandate. A survey of towns around the state found that 75 percent of the total cost of planned construction projects would be in projects valued at more than $1 million.

"Our members report that projects often simply don't get done when the Wicks and the prevailing wage factors amplify the cost of the project well beyond what anyone was expecting," said G. Jeffrey Haber, executive director of the Association of Towns. "Those projects are continually postponed or simply dropped."

Even if Albany is convinced that an idea is right (for instance, that multiple contracts are better than using a general contractor), what right does it have to impose that notion on Massapequa and Massena? State government can set its own policies for its own operations, and let localities do as their elected leaders see fit.

The asbestos scare still costs us

Governor Pataki has also proposed action on another mandate that drives up capital costs for no good reason—the state law that sets strict, needless rules on removal of asbestos from publicly owned facilities. Both OSHA standards and New York's law affecting privately owned buildings use less cumbersome, less costly standards. Those rules reflect the understanding that minimal exposure to asbestos poses virtually no health threat. Eliminating stricter standards that aren't needed would save taxpayers tens of millions of dollars a year. (Of course, the whole idea that we need to remove asbestos to protect the health of those working or living inside is fundamentally ridiculous, most scientists say.)

In the city of Johnstown (Fulton County), taxpayers were forced to spend some $50,000 to demolish a deteriorated

19th-century barn that contained asbestos. Mayor Bill Pollak says the demolition could have been done for a fraction of that cost, if not for the asbestos mandate from Albany.

"That's a crime, the money that's been flushed down the toilet," the mayor said.

In the city of Beacon, Mayor Clara Lou Gould says, applications for Community Development projects that involve asbestos "are usually left for the individual to do with other money, since it can be done at a much lower cost, and the reduced standards are still safe."

In 1993, New York City schools spent tens of millions of dollars to remove asbestos from classrooms, where there was no evidence that children or teachers were being harmed. The decision to interrupt classes for two weeks, in the absence of real danger, has been questioned.[46] The high cost of the removal, created by state mandates, made things even worse.

Costs for both public and private construction in New York are also driven needlessly high by an absurd liability law that assigns "absolute" liability to the owners of any construction site and contractors working there. Thus, even if a worker is drunk and violates express orders not to be on a construction site, if he is injured the property owner and contractor are legally to blame. Repeal of this so-called "safe place to work" law would help reduce construction costs for taxpayers as well as private individuals and businesses.

All told, reform of the prevailing-wage mandate, the Wicks Law, asbestos removal rules and liability laws could reduce local governments' costs for public construction by more than $1 billion.

"Businesses don't use multiple contracting as required for local governments under the Wicks Law, nor does the private sector have to comply with asbestos removal standards as restrictive as those applicable to local governments," Syracuse Mayor Roy Bernardi told the Legislature's fiscal committees in March 1999. "These indefensible mandates unnecessarily punish our already overburdened taxpayers."

---

[46] See, for instance, "The Great Asbestos Ripoff," *New York POST*, p. 26, February 12, 1999.

Chapter 4

Public Employment: Why Not the Best for New York?

New Yorkers want—and deserve—the best in public service. After all, we can't have high-quality transportation, health, sanitation, police, recreation and other services without high-quality men and women in the jobs that provide those services.

But mandates from Albany often act to degrade the quality of the public's employees, and thus the quality of public services.

To be sure, the great majority of government employees in New York are qualified, hardworking and dedicated to public service. At the local government level in particular, most New Yorkers would agree that the men and women who serve in police and fire departments, sanitation and public works agencies, and other municipal and school services do a good job, often under difficult circumstances. A proper concern that those workers receive the respect they deserve is all the more reason to make sure that less-than-satisfactory public employees are not tolerated.

Managers at all levels of government are severely limited in their ability to make the best use of human resources, because of New York's cumbersome civil service laws. More than a century ago, this system was created to protect both workers and the public from political and other abuses in government hiring and personnel practices. Yet in the last 30 years, our society has produced two other, powerful and overlapping influences that provide such protections.

First, public employees in state government and most municipalities and school districts are now unionized. That trend is partly a result of, and partly the cause of, various laws and regulatory practices enacted by governors and legislators. The state's Taylor Law, allowing unionization of public employees and prohibiting strikes by them, was enacted in 1967.

Second, laws enacted by Congress and decisions by judges in both federal and state courts have created broad new rights for all workers—whether unionized or not, in the private and public sectors alike. Statutes such as the Americans with Disabilities Act, Title VII of the Civil Rights Act, the Family and Medical Leave Act, and New York's own Human Rights Law were not on the books when the civil service system was created.

In other words, New York now has not one, not two, but *three* separate sets of laws and rules that tell public managers how to deal with employees. The combined effect is to put a straitjacket on management authority and accountability.

Given that, all three systems should be completely overhauled. At the least, Albany's civil-service mandates on *localities* should be abolished, and voters given the freedom to enact such rules in their local governments if they so choose.

How did we get here?

In 1883, after observing political favoritism and corruption in public employment, then-Assemblyman Theodore Roosevelt sponsored legislation to create a system of civil service under which public employees would be chosen based on merit. The law was embraced by Governor Grover Cleveland, and helped to create the good-government image that both leaders used in advancing to the Presidency. For decades, the civil-service system had an undeniably positive effect on public services in New York.

Like many other states, though, New York saw its civil service system change from an agent that improves public services as Teddy Roosevelt wanted to one that, in many cases, damages the services the public depends upon.

Governing magazine, which reports on states and localities around the country, wrote recently that, among outmoded civil service systems nationwide, "for decades, the king of the calcified and recalcitrant beasts has been the New York state civil service system, a monster off whose chest comprehensive reports on reform bounded like Wiffle balls—27 of them in all since the 1970s. For public managers in the Empire State, it was simply one of the larger complications of government service to be worked around on a regular basis."[47] Richard P. Nathan, director of the Nelson A. Rockefeller Institute of Government in Albany, wrote in 1993 that "New York represents an extreme" among rigid systems that prevent public administrators from exercising effective leadership.[48] And the Citizens Budget Commission commented: "The civil service system may be government's most notorious systemic barrier to efficiency and corruption...Rather than protect civil servants, the regulations restrict the motivation to be productive and competitive...Short of gross misconduct, there is little basis at present to remove a non-performing employee; the disciplinary process set forth by civil service rules (and, in many cases, reiterated in union contracts) is convoluted and slow."[49]

In the past four years, by all accounts, New York's civil service system has changed for the better.

Now, according to *Governing*'s Jonathan Walters, the state Civil Service Department "is becoming a place that actually values service over the status quo." In fact, the magazine named Governor Pataki's Civil Service Commissioner, George C. Sinott, one of its 1998 Public Officials of the Year for his leadership in turning things around.

Among other things, the new reforms included loosening of the "rule of three," which had required that government managers hire new workers from the top three scores on civil service exams. Both state and local officials complained that the rule often forced them to hire someone who did well on the test but was not the best qualified—especially for positions that do not attract many applicants. Under the state's new system, candidates are ranked on the basis of "band scoring," so that all scores from 96 to 100, for instance, will be considered equal.

"Using band scoring," the Civil Service Department said in an April 1998 publication, "improves hiring flexibility within

---

[47] "Untangling Albany," Jonathan Walters, *Governing*, December 1998.

[48] "Deregulating State and Local Government: What Can Leaders Do?", paper presented at Association for Public Policy Analysis and Management's Fourteenth Annual Research Conference, October 1993, Washington, D.C.

[49] *Budget 2000 Project: Restructuring Government Services*, December 1996; p. 39.

the existing requirements for merit and fitness selection by providing, at each score, a larger number of qualified and appointable candidates for State and local managers to consider for vacant positions."[50]

Since September 1997, according to the state Civil Service Department, most written exams for local government employees are band-scored in the same way as state exams. Exceptions are made for promotion examinations given to police, fire and corrections employees.

Many local officials say, though, that the reforms haven't helped them yet, partly because they often must deal with county-level civil service commissions that sometimes cling to the old ways.

'How can you provide services?'

"It doesn't test any human skills, like reliability or commitment," one town official in Westchester County said of the civil-service selection process.

Of employees chosen by the process, the official added: "They become permanent forever and you can't get rid of them. How can you provide services when you have such an arcane system?" Albany's reforms have had little impact on the flip side of the system—existing employees whom managers need to discipline or fire.

Jean Cochran, supervisor of the town of Southold (Suffolk County), recalls working for more than a year to deal with an employee who had missed 18 straight days of work. The employee, who had a drug abuse problem, was offered counseling but refused. Civil-service laws were among the reasons that dismissing the employee took so long, the supervisor said.

There are numerous other wrinkles that make the system difficult for government managers. Local officials have to master detailed rules over how many hours a part-time employee can work, how much he or she can be paid, and so on. The supervisor of one small town in the Binghamton area said he refuses to allow any full-time jobs on the town payroll, because complicated civil-service rules make it difficult for him to assure good public services. Instead,

---

[50] *Quality Standards/Innovative Applications: Award Winning Performance from New York State's* **New Civil Service**, New York State Department of Civil Service, April 1998.

employees who are, in effect, full-time are technically hired for two part-time jobs.

Civil service rules are not the only means to the desirable end of promoting good government. Much more than the federal or state governments, local governments are highly accountable for results. They're close to home. If the streets are not plowed, if the police don't do their job, or other essential services are not performed, people know it—and will voice their displeasure, ultimately through the voting booth.

One way to combine a move to *more efficient* government with continued assurance of *clean* government would be to (a) allow municipalities serving populations of less than, say, 100,000 to opt out of the civil service system entirely; and (b) require those taking the option to publish the names and positions of all newly hired individuals in local newspapers. Both moves would give more power to local voters. Municipalities could be required to seek voters' input through public hearings before going to merit-based selection; in cases where the citizenry expressed clear preference for the traditional approach, elected officials would no doubt honor that preference (or risk being thrown out in the next election). And residents would know from the listings of new hires whether the mayor was putting his family members, for instance, on the payroll.

Historically, New York State's leaders have given the public employee unions virtual veto power over any suggestions for change in the civil service system. That's fine for the unions, but it's often harmful to the taxpayers who depend on government services. It's time to put the people first.

The high cost of binding arbitration

In April 1999, a state-appointed arbitrator issued a decision in a contract dispute between Nassau County and the Superior Officers Association representing county police sergeants, lieutenants and captains. The police officers were among the highest-paid in the nation; the county was facing a major budget deficit; and inflation for the years covered by the contract was projected to average 2 to 3 percent a year.

The arbitrator's decision: a 24 percent pay increase over five years. A captain's base salary would jump from $90,783 to $117,114—not counting night differential, overtime and other stipends.

The Nassau County budget director called the decision "outrageous." The director of the local Citizen Budget Committee said it was "alarming" and "irresponsible." Standard & Poor's, the credit rating agency, said the pay increases raised new concern "over the county's ability to balance its budget on an ongoing basis."

Georgia leads the way on reform

Abolishing civil service rules isn't a new idea. In Georgia, Governor Zell Miller and the state Legislature enacted legislation to eliminate civil-service hiring and firing regulations for employees hired after July 1, 1996. In a 1997 review of the change, Governing summarized the law's impact this way:

> Early this year, two Georgia corrections officers were caught using cocaine. One was dismissed, but has appealed the dismissal. His case could drag on for as long as a year. If he wins, he may be reinstated with full back pay. The other has no such hopes. Within a matter of days, his case was reviewed and the dismissal was deemed justified. There will be no appeal. The difference isn't the offense, or the job history of the two officers...Officer "B" came in after the new law took effect.[51]

Public managers in Georgia have the freedom to do more than fire corrupt or inept employees. While basic pay and benefits are the same for all employees, now promotions, demotions, transfers and pay raises for newer hires can be made on the basis of performance—the way they usually are in private business.[52]

All across New York State, the public managers whom taxpayers have hired to deliver vital services wish they had the freedom to make decisions that way. Can there be any doubt that services would be better as a result?

---

[51] "Who Needs Civil Service?", *Governing*, August 1997, p. 17.

[52] The Center for Governmental Research Inc. has suggested that merit pay, one of the Georgia reforms, be considered for public employees in New York. "Negotiated labor contracts and graded/stepped salary schedules restrict managers' ability to recognize individual achievement," the center observed in a May 1992 report, *Restructuring the New York State Personnel/Civil Service System*, sponsored by the Upstate New York Roundtable on Manufacturing.

"No one begrudges the police a living wage," *Newsday* said in an editorial. "The problem here is a system that whipsaws police salaries upward without regard for taxpayers."[53]

The arbitrator's decision was one of 20 or so made each year under Section 209(4) of the state's Civil Service Law, enacted in 1974. The law requires binding arbitration, overseen by the state Public Employment Relations Board, in contract disputes where municipalities and their police or fire unions do not reach agreement. Most other public employees—teachers, sanitation workers and parks employees, for instance—do not have recourse to binding arbitration.

Police and fire unions say it's good public policy to force municipalities into arbitration of their contract disputes. Without the law, the only recourse for public safety workers would be to go on strike, they argue.[54] Yet state environmental conservation officers and prison guards do not benefit from binding arbitration; nor do county sheriff's deputies or guards in county or municipal jails.

Binding arbitration clearly has one benefit for police and fire union members, though: it gives them better raises than they would get without the mandate from Albany.

In 1990, wage increases decided through compulsory arbitration averaged just over 6 percent. During that year, the state's private-sector economy went into a tailspin, eliminating 145,000 jobs. The job hemorrhage continued in 1991, as 314,000 jobs disappeared. The economic disaster that befell the state led to lower salary increases under binding arbitration—to around 5.5 percent, still far above the 4.2 percent inflation rate.[55] State law enforcement officers received no raise in either 1991 or 1992.

In recent years, PERB and the arbitrators it approves have been more friendly to taxpayers.

"Salary increases awarded to local government police and fire departments during arbitration proceedings are starting to come down," the New York State Conference of Mayors said in a report on 1995 arbitration decisions. Average salary

---

[53] "Whipsaw: Cops deserve good pay but LI taxpayers deserve responsible salary decisions," May 5, 1999.

[54] See, for instance, *Binding Arbitration in New York State*, Decker Economics Associates, East Greenbush, N.Y., February 1999. The report was underwritten by the New York State Professional Firefighters Association.

[55] Data from *Binding Arbitration in New York State*.

awards declined from 4.2 percent in 1994 to 3.1 percent in 1995, 3.5 percent in 1996, 3.2 percent in 1997 and 3.3 percent in 1998, according to the association.

On the other hand, according to NYCOM, figuring inflation into the mix shows that there is still room to reduce awards. The average 1994 award of 4.2 percent was 2 percentage points above inflation. In 1995, arbitrators' awards were barely a quarter of 1 percent above the inflation level. In 1996, that differential was 0.5 percent; in 1997, 1.4 percent; and in 1998, 1.6 percent.[56]

In Buffalo, city officials estimate they could save $17 million in police and fire compensation if the binding arbitration mandate were repealed. Those dollars could be much better used to reduce taxes, and thereby attract more business and job growth; and/or improve services.

Other public employees, including thousands who work in public safety, negotiate contracts without binding arbitration. And, even ignoring the cost, it's yet another administrative headache for mayors, city managers and other officials who need to spend their time on issues other than dealing with Albany's mandates.

In the absence of repeal, requiring PERB to give stronger consideration to the taxpayers—as Governor Pataki has proposed repeatedly—would help. The Governor's proposal would require arbitrators to give first consideration to a municipality's ability to pay higher salaries without raising taxes.

Most cities around the state have struggled with economic and population decline for decades. In response, they've raised tax rates even in years when spending was held in check. Yet higher taxes, and loss of jobs and population, amount to a death spiral that will continue until municipal governments can reduce costs, cut taxes and become more attractive to both businesses and homeowners. Reducing the cost of Albany's binding arbitration mandate is one way to start turning the cities around.

Arbitrators should also be required to consider private-sector pay and benefit practices. After all, the factory worker and supermarket clerk pay public employees' salaries, through their tax dollars. Why shouldn't private-sector employees' raises (and their share of health insurance costs) influence the public sector?

---

[56] *Local Government Police and Fire Arbitration Awards Issued in 1998.* NYCOM used the Consumer Price Index for Urban Wage Earners and Clerical Workers to measure inflation.

Another way to reform binding arbitration, as the Citizen Budget Commission and others have suggested, is to require that it be preceded by binding "last best offer" rules, which require an arbitrator to choose one side's offer rather than a compromise. Such a system creates a powerful incentive for both sides to move to the middle ground.

Compensation for public-safety officials is another area, like social services, where state leaders imposed new costs on taxpayers during the 1999 session.

Section 207-m of the state's General Municipal Law requires that a chief of police must be given at least the same salary increase given to his or her highest-ranking subordinate. In 1999, the Legislature approved and Governor Pataki signed a measure that will require police chiefs be given an increase in *fringe benefits* equal to any such increase for the next-highest official in the department.

Other laws that hurt taxpayers

Other mandates in state law, created at the behest of public employee unions, also drive up police and fire costs, and translate into higher local taxes.

For instance, Section 207-a(2) of the General Municipal Law says that a firefighter who receives a work-related disability pension is also eligible for a supplemental municipal pension in most instances. That supplemental payment must be increased whenever the base pay of the position from which the firefighter has retired is increased. These supplemental pensions cost municipalities around the state $14 million in 1997, according to the Conference of Mayors.

Certainly, firefighters perform a valuable, often heroic service. Those who are injured on the job—especially those who are hurt during an actual fire—deserve generous compensation. In fact, Section 207-a(2) originated as protection for firefighters who suffered traumatic injury in the line of duty. Now, as a result of court decisions, the mandate applies to injuries such as back pain caused by falling from a chair in the firehouse.

With such a loose eligibility standard, at different times in recent years the city of Rochester was giving disability payments to 64 firefighters, more than 10 percent of its force; and Mount Vernon had 23 firefighters on disability, from a total of 130. In Oneonta, with a smaller force, city taxpayers spend $80,000 a year for three firefighters out on disability. Clearly, the rules for disability retirement awards need to be tightened.

What would be the effect of major changes to the civil service law and other mandates on how public managers deal with employees? Better public services, for one. Mayors, town supervisors, municipal department heads and other managers—as well as employees—would be able to focus more on quality of services rather than bureaucratic rules.

And the savings to taxpayers could be huge. Payrolls for counties, municipalities and school districts across New York State totaled more than $17 billion in 1997. This state's local government bureaucracy is far bigger, in comparison to population, than those in other states. As countless employers in the private sector have seen, cutting bureaucracy and extra layers of management allow for better products and services *with fewer workers*. Reducing local government payrolls by an average of 5 percent would provide savings of $1 billion or more, including the cost of benefits.

Time to review the Taylor Law

When it was enacted in 1967, New York State's Taylor Law was hailed by state leaders and public-employee unions as a model for modern labor relations in the public sector. And it clearly has created more labor stability in the public sector, at both the state and local levels.

Just as clearly, though, the law is imperfect. The mandates and inefficiencies it imposes on municipal officials drive up costs and make delivery of quality public services more difficult.

The Taylor Law doesn't even meet its stated goal of preventing strikes by public-employee unions. Teachers' union members in Yonkers went on strike in September 1999—forcing children to stay home, starting the school year with chaos and creating a nightmare for parents. The strike was effective in forcing the school district into concessions sought by the union—*precisely the type of tactic the Taylor Law is supposed to prevent*. The Civil Service Employees Association openly brags about the power of strikes to bolster the union's negotiating power.[57]

---

[57] A history of the union, posted on its website, says: "Summer, 1975: One thousand Dutchess County employees stage a one-week walkout. Their strike, the first-ever by county employees, attracts national attention. The result? Members win a better contract which they overwhelmingly ratify." See *http://www.cseainc.org/yesterdy.html*.

One of the chief flaws of government at all levels is its tendency to pass laws, brag about them, and then ignore the results. There is no denying that the Taylor Law has had a major impact on government—and thus the quality and cost of public services—in New York State. More than three decades after its enactment, it's time to consider whether it works *for all New Yorkers,* not just the unions.

Among other things, such a review should compare compensation and work rules in the public sector to those in the private sector, and at different levels of government. For instance, arbitration awards for local government unions often exceed wage increases enjoyed by state employees—perhaps the Taylor Law should prohibit such inequities.

Chapter 5

The Cost of Liability, And Other Mandates

On Memorial Day 1992, Virgil and John Brown were visiting a Coney Island pier when Virgil decided to go for a swim. He climbed over a wooden railing, and leaped 15 feet into the water.

Tragically, the water next to the pier in New York Bay was only five feet deep. Virgil Brown suffered a paralyzing injury. When John saw his brother helpless in the water, he dove in—and ended up paralyzed as well. Both now need permanent care. If their families are unable to pay for such care, taxpayer-funded Medicaid and other programs will provide it.

But a Brooklyn jury decided taxpayer-funded care for as long as the men need it is not enough. Because New York City did not post signs warning against diving from the pier, the jury found, city taxpayers should pay $104 million to compensate the Browns for their injuries. Should the men have been expected to be more cautious about jumping into unknown waters? Under New York's liability laws, it didn't really matter.

"That $100 million now due the Browns could hire 1,500 teachers, or 1,250 police officers, fire fighters or correction officers," the *New York Post* commented in an editorial after the jury award. "How many *won't* be hired if this award is *not* reduced on appeal?"[58]

New York City residents—and those in every other area of the Empire State—suffer under a liability system that encourages lawsuits against anyone whom trial lawyers perceive to

---

[58] "A 7,500,002-Person Tragedy," April 12, 1998.

have "deep pockets." The lawyers have gone so far as to create something called the Big Apple Pothole and Sidewalk Protection Corporation, which makes it easier for them to sue the city when someone trips or slips on a sidewalk and suffers an injury. The city will pay more than $400 million in claims for fiscal year 1999, city Comptroller Alan Hevesi estimates; most of those are for personal injuries.

Small municipalities get hit, too. In Saratoga County, the town of Greenfield was threatened with a $1 million lawsuit after a man was hurt while sledding on a town-owned hill. And in the nearby town of Clifton Park, a local resident sued the volunteer ambulance squad and the town government for $5 million, for what *The Daily Gazette* of Schenectady said was "taking too long trying to save his life." The emergency workers spent a few minutes trying to stabilize the patient, who had suffered an epileptic seizure.

"Just who is the $5 million supposed to come from, anyway?" *The Daily Gazette* editorialized. "The ambulance company, which doesn't have it, and whose insurance might not cover all of it? In that case, the company might have to shut down ...The towns of Clifton Park and Ballston were also named in the lawsuit, on the deep-pocket theory of litigation. But why should taxpayers in those towns have to pay?"[59]

They have to pay because of state laws that allow local governments—small towns, as well as the Big Apple—to be sued for 100 percent of damages even if they bear only 1 percent of the responsibility for a tragedy. The legal principle underpinning such suits is called joint-and-several liability, and is one of the central targets of a broad-based coalition known as New Yorkers for Civil Justice Reform. The coalition includes numerous local governments around the state, as well as the statewide associations representing them in Albany.

Asking the Legislature earlier this year to repeal the Wicks Law and other mandates, New York City Mayor Rudolph Giuliani called reform of the state's civil justice laws "another critical mandate relief item." He said: "Tort reform would enable the city to continue to compensate injured parties reasonably while preventing tort costs from escalating uncontrollably." In particular, the Mayor urged "a reasonable cap" of $250,000 on pain-and-suffering awards. He also

---

[59] "You can't sue everybody," July 1, 1998.

urged creation of a minimum medical expense threshold of $5,000 for plaintiffs seeking non-economic damages, to prevent major awards to claimants with minor injuries.[60]

Another idea is to include lawsuits against municipalities within the jurisdiction of the state's Court of Claims. The court is the sole trial court for claims against state government. It was created to eliminate unfair jury decisions against taxpayers and to promote uniformity in the resolution of liability claims against the state. The same factors argue for including municipalities, as does the rising tide of outrageous judgments against municipal taxpayers.

Emergency services suffer

The liability issue is one reason volunteer fire and ambulance companies across New York are struggling.

Another is that Albany has imposed training mandates that make it harder for the services to attract the volunteers on which they rely.

"Ambulance crews are struggling with volunteer shortages, especially during weekday shifts," the Albany *Times Union* reported after an in-depth investigation. The shortage, it said, has contributed to longer waiting times for ambulances to arrive—and even, in some cases, deaths.[61]

The growing shortages create "serious implications for the response times of rural ambulance crews, who are already slowed by having to respond from home or work and having to travel long distances on country roads," the newspaper reported. "Sometimes, squads don't have enough volunteers to respond at all, so calls roll to neighboring agencies. Occasionally, calls will roll to a third or fourth agency, costing precious minutes as more pagers sound and other crews see how many people will respond."

Some emergency squads around the state have responded by charging or raising fees so they can hire crew members, especially during daytime hours. But, according to the *Times Union*: "Other squads are reluctant to charge people in their community. 'We have some people in town who have no

---

[60] Testimony to Senate Finance Committee and Assembly Ways and Means Committee, February 2, 1999.

[61] "Another kind of emergency: volunteer shortage," June 13, 1999.

insurance and if we sent them a bill they would not buy food—they would pay the bill,' said Shirley Ainsworth, captain of the Providence Volunteer Ambulance Corps."

Suburban towns are affected, too. In fact, the Association of Towns has made easing mandates on volunteer services one of its top requests for action by the Governor and the Legislature.

"This could drive property tax rates out of sight," association Executive Director G. Jeffrey Haber said. "Let's look at this before we can't afford to live in New York State anymore." Haber, a longtime member of a volunteer squad in Rensselaer County, believes the tougher mandates may harm, rather than promote, public safety. The association urged state leaders "to review existing training requirements, and to restructure those mandates in a manner that would sustain and encourage volunteerism in New York's municipalities."

The list of seemingly wasteful state mandates on localities goes on and on. Some other examples:

- The state's Commission on Correction dictates the details of jail construction by counties around the state. Its mandates have added significantly to the cost local taxpayers must incur for such projects. The commission has also narrowly interpreted the state Constitution as blocking counties from sharing jails.

- State bidding laws require municipalities to solicit competitive bids for contracts and purchases over certain amounts that were set years ago. Now, in many cases, those amounts are so low that they effectively stand in the way of efficient purchasing rather than encouraging good government. It's probably time to raise the levels, substantially.

- Then there are the mandates that seem almost frivolous, but reinforce the general attitude that Albany must tell local officials exactly what to do. For instance, Section 124 of the General Municipal Law, enacted in 1976, requires that all elevators in buildings in Nassau County shall be inspected periodically "for the purposes of public safety." Cities, towns and villages in the county were thereby required to assure that installation, operation and maintenance of elevators be at least as stringent as the relevant provisions of the state building code already in force. In other words, elevator riders in Nassau County are protected by a law that says another law must be enforced.

Leverage, don't mandate, local efficiency

The Governor and the Legislature *can* promote better, more efficient government at the local level without imposing mandates—by using the state's enormous financial strength to leverage action by localities.

Of the $73.3 billion in this year's state budget, roughly two-thirds goes to local public schools, counties and New York City for social services programs, and to municipalities for general financial support, transportation and other purposes. While much of that comes from Washington and is subject to federal mandates, more than $20 billion of the total is directly from New Yorkers' state taxes and mainly governed by decisions made in Albany. That figure includes state school aid, general revenue sharing and social-services spending not subject to federal mandate.

For all the perpetual rhetoric about improving schools and other public services, the state does little by way of creating real incentives for localities and school districts to improve. Perhaps the single biggest effort along these lines is the school report cards that Education Commissioner Mills and the Regents have created. The report cards generate strong incentives for school districts to improve, by virtue of the public attention paid to hard data about performance of individual schools.

Albany could do more to shine a spotlight on the performance of localities and schools. For example, the Office of the State Comptroller publishes annual reports on the finances of every school district and municipality. OSC should consider including data on per-capita taxes and spending for each unit of government, along with tables showing how much those figures increase or decrease from year to year. The results would surely be noticed.

Another powerful way to encourage taxpayer-friendly performance is to build incentives into every aid program in Albany. Why not give more aid to localities that reduce their costs—and less to those that do not? Such incentives should reward, for instance, those localities that decrease taxpayer costs through privatization or other forms of competitive contracting. "It is clear that the incidence of contracting is increasing in local governments and that local officials generally are satisfied with doing it," a public-management expert from the University of Southern California reported in a leading professional journal recently.

"The research evidence reviewed demonstrates that contracting improves efficiency, improves effectiveness, or results in cost savings in the fields of debt collection, electric services, fire protection, housing construction, parks, payroll and data processing, public works, recreation, solid waste collection, transit, wastewater treatment, water supply, and multiple services," the USC professor wrote. "Contracting has been less effective or ineffective in the fields of human service and property assessment."[62]

Time to end 'political sprawl'

Local government leaders in New York are not the only ones who are angry at the imposition of mandates from above. The former mayor of Rutland, Vermont, Jeff Wennberg, is, too. He calls the problem "political sprawl."

"Just as commercial sprawl robs us of our sense of place, political sprawl robs us of our sense of community," Mayor Wennberg writes. "It denies us the opportunity to choose our own course and it cheats us of the obligation to solve our own problems, citizen to citizen. The early settlers well exercised their muscles of local interdependence. Ours are in a state of advancing atrophy. And when we fail to exercise these skills, we fall apart from one another.

"Every thing the state decides for us is one less thing we are allowed to decide for ourselves," Wennberg says. "If the state sees no impediment to mandating dog license fees, what aspect of local governance is beyond their reach?"[63]

Before state policy makers enact mandates that are intended to make local governments work better, they should consider the Hippocratic oath for physicians: First, do no harm. State mandates do *a lot* of harm, by driving up costs and rendering public services less effective. It's time for a change.

---

[62] Gilbert B. Siegel, "Where Are We On Local Government Service Contracting?", *Public Productivity & Management Review*, Vo. 22 No. 3, March 1999.

[63] See *http://www.vermontgop.org/jeff_w5.htm*.

Chapter 6

Recommendations, and the Savings Taxpayers Can Reap

The problem of costly and inefficient state mandates requires a number of solutions.

The sooner state leaders enact those changes, the sooner New Yorkers will enjoy the better and more effective services they deserve in schools, police and fire departments, and other local government operations. The more completely Governor Pataki and the Legislature attack mandates, the more local officials can reduce costs and cut taxes—and the more the state's economy will grow as a result.

The mandate-relief agenda includes the following major steps:

To improve the schools:

- Move decision-making authority from Albany to the schools by repealing the Triborough Amendment, and rethinking laws that mandate detailed aspects of curriculum.

- Promote teachers' and administrators' lifetime commitment to quality by repealing or dramatically reforming tenure. In addition, the state Education Department should fulfill the requirements of existing law by reporting annually on teacher and administrator performance; and school districts should more effectively use existing procedures to evaluate and react to such performance.

- New York's special education laws and regulations must be reformed further, to reduce costs and encourage students to reach their full potential.

Potential savings for local taxpayers: $150 million.

To make social welfare programs more affordable, and more fair:

- Cut administrative costs by streamlining the duplicative combination of state and local bureaucracies overseeing welfare, Medicaid and other social services.

- Reduce costs in Medicaid's acute-care program by eliminating the graduate medical education tax, reducing reimbursements to providers and taking other steps.

- Reform Medicaid's long-term care program by encouraging more family support of such costs, creating more competition for long-term care providers and taking other steps.

- Devote localities' savings from welfare reform to reducing taxes rather than increasing spending.

Potential savings for local taxpayers: $2.3 billion.

To make public construction more efficient and less costly:

- Make New York's prevailing-wage law truly reflect "prevailing" wages in a community—using union contract rules only when union workers are in the majority locally. Other reforms could include allowing municipalities to enact their own prevailing-wage laws that meet the requirements of the state Constitution; and creating thresholds below which the rules would not apply.

- Repeal the Wicks Law, allowing taxpayers to benefit from more efficient and less costly construction procedures used on most private-sector projects.

- Rewrite the law governing asbestos removal in public facilities, to match practices used by the federal government and in the private sector. And, repeal the "safe place to work" law that imposes senseless liability costs on both public and private building projects.

Potential savings for local taxpayers: $1 billion.

To give public managers the ability to hire and keep the best workforce:

- Repeal or radically reform civil service laws to restore their original promise of promoting better government.

- Repeal the binding-arbitration mandate so real negotiations, rather than state-imposed settlements, decide pay disputes between local governments and public safety employees.

- Reform disability laws governing injured firefighters so the rules apply to injures that occur during actual duty.

- Take a fresh look at the state's Taylor Law, more than 30 years after its enactment.

Potential savings for local taxpayers: $1 billion.

To cut costs and promote better public services generally:

- Reform New York's outmoded liability laws to eliminate frivolous "deep-pocket" lawsuits against municipalities and other institutions.

- Reconsider mandates on emergency services that discourage potential volunteers.

- Rewrite state aid formulas for schools and municipalities to encourage privatization and innovation.

Potential savings for local taxpayers: $800 million.

The proposals above add up to more than $5 billion in savings for taxpayers.

In addition to the savings from mandate relief and new incentives for innovation at the local level, New York City and the state's 57 other counties should devote most, if not all, of their tobacco settlement revenues to tax relief. That would produce additional hundreds of millions of dollars' reduction in property taxes, and other local taxes.

The effect of all these changes would be an immediate, major improvement in New York State's competitive standing. That, in turn, would lead to more growth, and more jobs. If there is any mandate that voters have given leaders in Albany, that's it.

Index

T

U

V

W